INCREMENTAL COURAGE

By

WARREN CHRISTOPHER

Warren Christopher

Table of Contents

Warren Christopher

About the Author

Warren Christopher is a first-time author. He is a combat veteran who served nearly twenty-five years in the U.S. Army. His tours of duty included assignments in Europe, Asia, Hawaii, and throughout the continental United States. Warren's combat tours included Kosovo, Bosnia, Iraq, the Philippines, and Afghanistan.

He has served in high-profile assignments including commander, speechwriter, aide-de-camp, congressional liaison, Pentagon staff officer, and human resources officer.

Warren is a doting father to two amazing daughters, a graduate of Purdue University, has a master's degree from Marine Corps University, and an executive MBA from the University of Georgia. As a lifelong learner, Warren is currently pursuing a

Doctorate in Business Administration at Drexel University.

Warren is a first-generation college graduate and has committed his life to public service. After retiring from the U.S. Army, he served as a chief of staff and a senior policy advisor for federal executive branch agencies. Warren also sought nomination for representative in Congress in Maryland. He is a small business owner and has served honorably on several prominent boards. One of his proudest and fondest contributions is as a mentor with Big Brothers Big Sisters, National Capital Area (BBBSNCA).

Acknowledgements

❖ I dedicate this work to my daughters, Brittany and Ashley. You are the reason I live. I love you more than words could ever convey.

❖ To my ex-wife, Lisa. Thanks for helping make it possible for me to be a dad, and thanks for your friendship.

❖ Pops, I love you, and thank God I have a dad!

❖ To all those souls who impacted my life and helped set the conditions for my contributions to the world, I am eternally grateful! Your mentorship, advocacy, generosity, and kindness has made all the difference. I honor you always.

❖ To my Columbus, Georgia crew and family, my military brethren, my friends, and mentees, I love you.

❖ To my spiritual leaders, thank you for your nurturing and teachings.

❖ Lastly, to my beloved Madea, my Big Dad, aunts, uncles, siblings, and cousins... thank you!

Warren Christopher

Preface

Confronting one's pain, failures, hurt, and disappointments takes courage.

In this work, I share a number of challenging situations and experiences that almost broke me at an early age. To move forward, I had to lean on my faith, unlearn some stuff, consider a new perspective, be vulnerable, and develop the courage to confront and slay my demons. The masks I wore, the pretending I did, and the anger I carried blocked my blessings and my peace and delayed my God-ordained destiny.

The level of transparency I exercise might be shocking to you. I will reveal things that may be trigger issues to those who have experienced trauma, especially sexual trauma.

In the words of Franklin D. Roosevelt, "Courage is not the absence of fear, but rather the assessment that something else is more important than fear."

The only thing more powerful than fear is courage. Along the way, I've gained courage incrementally in all areas of my life, and that has made all the difference. In the passages ahead, I'll share the experiences that forged me into a courageous man. These experiences, and the actions I took, helped move me to a higher level of consciousness. I invite you to consider my perspective on courage, and how I came to be the man I am today. There are many aspects of courage I've become intimately familiar with. Here are but a few significant areas I learned to fully embrace.

❖ The courage to not assimilate.

❖ The courage to do what's right, even when no one is looking.

❖ The courage to follow a dream—to jump. I got bruised, scratched, and scraped, but at least I jumped.

❖ The courage to speak up and stand up for the voiceless and the most vulnerable who were too weak to stand on their own.

❖ The courage I had as a child was very different than the courage I have as an adult. As a child, I was expected to be seen and not heard.

❖ The courage I possessed as a lieutenant was

vastly different from the courage I carried as a lieutenant colonel.

❖ The courage to be unapologetically Black and *me*.

❖ The courage to be a dad on days when I thought I didn't have the fortitude to stand, even though I didn't have a model.

❖ The courage to divorce religion and establish a personal relationship with the spirit of God.

❖ The courage to speak about my pain and get the mental health treatment I needed to be able to run my race.

❖ The courage to be vulnerable and self-aware.

❖ The courage to speak my truth without being indignant, defensive, or angry☐.

❖ The courage to *live*—not according to how others thought I should live, but rather, in line with the life God has ordained for me.

❖ The courage to challenge my intellectual fears and believe in myself.

Much of what I share will not be accommodating or convenient; my sharing may be chilling. It will challenge you and cause significant reflection and consideration.

Incremental Courage...

"Humans are not built in silence, but in word, in work, in action-reflection." (Paulo Freire)

Warren Christopher

A Letter to My Younger Self

Dear Chris,

In the beginning, there was light...and darkness! Life threw you lemons, and you found honey and made lemonade. You showed amazing strength, courage, and willpower. You commanded the light to shine brighter during a time of great void.

There were many times you had to ask yourself, "So what? This is what has happened, so what am I gonna do about it?" You refused to wallow in pity or to be defeated. Your grit and tenacity still amaze me! I am the person I am today because of your steadfastness and honor.

You were so strong, even in the face of what seemed to be insurmountable challenges. Because of your strength, character, and spirituality, we survived! Before long, we were thriving. And now, because of the foundation you laid for us, coupled with the mercy and grace of God, we are soaring! Because of your courage, my season traveling alone was met with supernatural growth, sage wisdom, and keen discernment—you made me a better person! As I reflect, I've come to appreciate and value my uniqueness. I am unapologetically me because of you! Your experiences from yesterday—good, bad, and indifferent—made me the unwavering man I am today!

Grandmama did a marvelous job raising you! Although she didn't show much affection or tender nurturing, she instilled in you dignity, loyalty, faithfulness, respect, discipline, kindness, gratitude, and humility. Moreover, she taught you decency—to be a person of your word and to respect your elders. She taught you to do what's right, even when no one is looking, to have integrity above reproach, and to be loyal and true to yourself. She also taught you to treat all people with dignity and respect, regardless of their social status, possessions, or race—and not to take any wooden nickels. She taught you responsibility and accountability during the countless months of just you and Grandmama working on the farm in L.A. (that's "lower Alabama," not "Los Angeles," LOL □), all while wishing you were in summer school or some magical place far, far away—or even doing homework, LOL and SMDH □□♂□□. Oh, and those whoopins—they were necessary and proved to be very effective! In a different way, Grandmama taught you love and to garner self-enthusiasm and avoid being discouraged when you could have very well done otherwise. She taught you to dream. Because of this, I've had big dreams again and again.

We find great joy and fulfillment in serving mankind. Together, we've served our country, our community, and our family with dignity and honor. We've poured goodness into the lives of many, and for that, God has continued to show us tremendous and unprecedented favor and mercy. We've achieved beyond our dreams, and God has honored the prayers you prayed so fervently and faithfully—we find great strength in our faith.

Through it all, you were quite ambitious. We've

visited nearly every continent, traveled to nearly every state in the U.S., sailed many oceans, and even came close to touching the stars and moon during thousands of flights. We've kept company with world leaders, royalty, celebrities, and the humblest of God's profound creation. Our life experiences blow people's minds, especially when I tell them about you!

It's only because of the courage you developed that I was able to confront and address life's bitter moments. Because of your resilience, I found relief through my spirituality. By the mercy and grace of God, I found relief through mental health treatment. We've attained Godly peace, little boy, and I'm guarding it with every power I possess. I learned our healing was in my vulnerability. I have a renewed mind and a sense of new birth.

Speaking of birth—I'm a dad! Because of your compassion, God granted me the gift of a daughter. Her name is Ashley, and I love her with all my being. I've imparted many of the attributes instilled in us by Grandmama on to my daughter. You would be very proud of how I protected and shielded her from the pain and disconnectedness you experienced. She *reminds me so much of you. She has your eyes, skin color, curiosity, and brains, LOL □. She's my twin!*

In 1996, shortly after I became a dad, I sought out to find our biological dad. I located him through a daytime TV talk show—the Ricki Lake Show. Ricki used to help reunite estranged family members, and she helped me find our dad. His name is Ben, and he's also from Alabama—Birmingham. I think I now understand your deep and early sense of service. Our dad served our country before we did. He was also a soldier—an engineer in the U.S. Army, and a decorated combat veteran. I guess the apple doesn't fall far from the tree, LOL □! Finding our dad meant we inherited siblings, with whom I enjoy a healthy and vibrant relationship, as I do with Pops—he's been a good mentor to me.

I've also mentored many people—young girls and boys, as well as adults. Of extraordinarily special note is a young man I've been a Big Brother to, whose name is Mason David! Mason and I met in 2012 through this amazing organization, Big Brothers Big Sisters (BBBS-NCA) in Washington, DC. Mason is a star! He has graduated from high school and is headed to college. He is very smart, responsible, respectful, kind, and extraordinarily helpful to his mom, who is a very nice and jovial lady. Through no fault of her own, she's a person with disabilities, and Mason is so supportive. At a very early age, he became a primary caregiver to his mom. He's also the most awesome big brother and support system for his younger sister, while balancing all of his interests and schoolwork. Mason is like a son to me; I am his keeper and will do all I can to aide his inevitable success. I will be forever grateful and indebted to BBBS because they allowed me to positively impact Mason in so many ways and pour goodness into his pitcher of life. I dedicate all my mentoring efforts to you, as I know you wish someone had cared for and shared time with you in that way when we were young!

I honor you from the top of my heart because that's where the good blood flows. I love you, and I'm forever indebted to you for providing a strong and unwavering foundation of strength, empathy, humility, honor, gratitude, and courage. Well, it's nearing time for me to go, but I want you to know you *set me up for a lifetime of joy, elation, and thanksgiving! I know you don't like to be singled out. This time, though, my friend, you deserve it! I'll carry you in my heart all my days. I wish you continued joy, love, and peace. My vision for you is to continue allowing God to order your steps and guide your spirit. You still have lots of impact to make... let's get to it!*

Love always,
Your Older Self □□□□□

Wildman Bottom—Where it All Started

Deep in southeast Alabama, on a huge family farm off a narrow red dirt road, was my street, Wildman Bottom Road. My aunts named the winding, rocky road, which connected to the lightly traveled county route and led to our house, deep down in the woods where we believed unknown creatures lived. There wasn't a single streetlight anywhere on this two-mile stretch. Lightning bugs were the closest thing we had to streetlights. Everyone called me Chris. Truthfully, I didn't even know my legal first name was Warren until much later, when I entered high school, LOL □ while SMDH □□♂□! My aunts often joked—although us kids didn't know it was a joke at the time—they would put us out on the road for the wild hyenas if we were disobedient. The farm was so big there seemed to be fields of produce for miles. There were also huge fields of apple, pear, and peach orchards and miles of pastures that were home to hundreds of cattle, sheep, goats, and horses. We also had multiple large pens of pigs and coops of chickens and bitties. Not to mention all the dogs with lots of puppies. There were no hired hands. We did all the work!

I attended preschool through first grade at Saint Joseph Catholic School in Holy Trinity, Alabama. I remember I loved school because I had the best early education teachers in the world: Ms. Bunnie Mac Cartcr and Ms. Thclma Kclly. They were absolutely the *best*! Those two teachers showed me so much care, love, and appropriate affection. Though they were quite strict, a paddle on the knuckles was also met with love, kindness, and a hug that said, "You know I love you, now get to your seat, do your work, and close your mouth." If I could've, I would've stayed at school all day, every day. I wanted to go to school year-round to avoid shelling butter beans and peas, picking grass from between tender crops, slopping hogs, feeding chickens ☐, baling hay, cutting grass...I mean, *damn*! And on top of all that, my aunts made me and my cousins pick leaves ☐ as a means to pay for our breakfast—an attempt to reinforce our ability to count.

In preschool, I loved learning, whether it was learning my numbers and letters or reading and writing. It was so much fun. Ms. Kelly would divvy out the leftover cut-up grilled cheese sandwich bites from breakfast as a prize for reading without hesitating or stumbling over words. I got lots of bites because I could read and write quite well. Those bites were so tasty. They were made by the cafeteria lady, Ms. Hubert. She also made scrambled eggs that could have been clouds, OMG ☐. They were light, fluffy, and the taste—simply sublime!

Though tough, my early education teachers were magical. They enforced strict classroom management and discipline while showing us so much love. I shall carry them, and the many lessons they taught me, in my heart and spirit forever. They were the epitome of excellence! I didn't understand until much later that the foundation of everything I needed to know in life, I learned in kindergarten: follow directions, clean up behind yourself, and treat people how they ought to be treated, with dignity and respect.

I had several other early childhood education teachers—they were nuns, and they were much stricter than Ms. Kelly and Ms. Bunnie Mae. In particular, Sister Mary Alice-Christine...OMG □. She taught music and put up with no foolishness at all. When it was time to learn "He's Got the Whole World in His Hands," you'd better not do anything but pay attention and sing. You see, I went to school during an era where spanking, paddling, and other forms of physical punishment were permitted and used often. Every infraction was met with a consequence, and boy, we did not want any consequences at the hands of the Catholic sisters. In hindsight, those consequences were very effective for me, as I suspect they were for many other rambunctious boys. Another one of my favorite songs was "They'll Know We Are Christians by Our Love." The lyrics definitely didn't include "by our possessions, our traditions, our status, and our ideologies."

Though I had a very challenging early childhood experience, my grandmama, "Madea," introduced me to religion straight out of the womb, LOL □. I was born premature on the family farm, delivered by Madea in a dilapidated, five-room shotgun house with a leaky tin roof. I recall stories from her about not expecting me to live. She told me later that she wrapped me in salve clothes, and my journey to the beginning of a healthy life started while sleeping in those salve clothes in the bed between my Madea and my "Big Dad" Warren, my namesake. You talk about praying—in the words of Dorothy Norwood, "My mother prayed for me, had me on her mind, she took the time and prayed for me. I'm so glad she prayed, I'm so glad she prayed for me."

My Madea stood about five foot, ten inches tall, weighing in at about 150 pounds. She had a complexion resembling the texture of milk chocolate, with thin, soft hair. As long as I was around her, I never saw her with any gray hair, although she always wore wigs in public. She was an only child. My Big Dad stood about six feet tall. He had salt and peppa' hair, a muscular build, and the complexion of a fair-skinned, mixed-race man. He had lots of sisters and brothers. You see, my granddaddy, the very best in the whole wide world, was the son of a White man. My Madea caught hell from his momma—"Muh-Muh," we affectionately called her. Back then, there were a lot of "brown paper bag" tests going on, including in my own family. I'll tell you more about that later, because I'd be directly affected by the brown paper bag standard myself.

My Big Dad was a civil engineer at Fort Benning, GA. Every Friday, on his way home from work, he'd stop and buy a large bag of penny candies and bubble gum. When he got home, he summoned us kids to the front porch, calling each of us by the nickname he'd assigned—mine was Flamp, LOL ☐. Many of the nicknames he gave us were inspired by characters from some of his favorite TV shows, like *Gun Smoke*, *Bonanza*, *Green Acres*, and *Lassie*. In his own subtle way, he was so loving, compassionate, and honorable. I was around eight years old when he died at home of natural causes. He was very healthy, so his sudden death shocked us all. I have never been more saddened by the loss of a loved one—I still miss him terribly! My grandmother was certainly the matriarch of the family. She and my grandfather were married for decades.

My grandfather used to tell me, "You can't control a lot of things in this world, but you can control your words and how you respond. Let your words be your bond." He instilled principles in me that I still live by today. I do my best, and I try to treat people as they ought to be treated—with dignity and respect. Like with my grandparents, family is hugely important to me. I really try to be true to my word, and I cultivate family ties every opportunity I get. I don't get it right every day, but I really try.

My mother was five foot, seven inches tall, and weighed about 130 pounds. She was fair-skinned and extremely beautiful, with flowing curly hair. She had seven children, four before me and two after me. However, I was the only one of her children left on the farm in the country to be raised by Madea and her three younger daughters, Auntie Miss,

Auntie VJ, and Auntie Faye, as well as Madea's middle son, Uncle Bud. My other aunts and uncles, Pat, Francis (Shug), Bull (Charlie), and Son (Gabe) also played a pivotal role in my upbringing. Times were tough emotionally. In that lonely place, feeling abandoned like a seed in the dark, wet, cold ground, all alone and unloved, I cried more days than I laughed. I was made fun of by my own family for being Black—or at least, darker than the other children. You see, many of my aunts and uncles, including my great aunts and uncles, were quite fair skinned. I am the product of an extra-marital affair, and my dad is very dark skinned. My younger aunts told me that my being darker than the others was the main reason my momma didn't want me. I'm not sure what the other reasons were.

My momma is now deceased. She never apologized, and she never talked to me about her "why"—she always pretended like she was without fault. I remember visiting her when she lived in the Elizabeth Canny public housing projects. My Madea, Uncle Bud, and I were headed home to the country and stopped by to see her. She wasn't home, but my siblings knew my Madea had taken legal guardianship over me. They told their neighbors I was their uncle. Later, on another occasion, I heard my momma tell people I wasn't hers, that I was her momma's child, SMDH 🤦‍♂️. During one of those visits, I also recall overhearing my momma's husband saying I wasn't his child, and he didn't want me carrying his last name. As soon as I could, I legally changed my last name. I never wanted to carry his name anyway! When my youngest and most favored Aunt Faye died, I remember my momma criticizing my dead aunt about how she raised her only daughter. My momma went on to say, "I raised all my kids well." Hearing that, it took everything I had within me not to scold her and unleash a lifetime of rage and painful emotions on her. I chose to maintain my peace. It appeared my momma never experienced any fulfilment in life. She seemed to always be at the center of confusion in family matters and often spoke ill of her own siblings.

I didn't come from an influential family in the sense of finances, but by the grace and favor of God,

I saw measure pressed down, shaken together, and running over. I vividly remember the summers at Madea's house. It was a season of harvest, revivals, and togetherness. Every summer, my cousins from Detroit, and sometimes from Ohio and other places in Alabama, and my siblings, who lived in Columbus, Georgia, with our mom, came to the country for the summer to help Grandmama on the family farm. I had more than twenty cousins.

During the summer months, on weekdays—and even on the weekends—we had to get up with the chickens, clean up, and go outside. I remember asking to come into the house to get a cold drink of water. My Aunt Faye would reply, "Drink out the water hose." That water was so hot I may as well have drank coffee □. To pass time on hot summer days, we snuck off to the watering hole for a swim, for which we were beaten mercilessly. That creek was infested with snakes and who knows what else—we were either fearless or stupid, LOL □. We also snuck off into the tall weeds and smoked rabbit tobacco. My cousins and I would take a brown paper bag, tear it into wide strips of paper, take

31

several pieces of the whole leaf □ of tobacco, roll it up, and smoke. Absolute novices trying to inhale, we choked and vomited, and our chests burned like hell, LOL. After each trial, we'd swear we would never do that again...until the next time, LMBAO. After trying that tobacco several times, I didn't smoke again 'til years later—and that was a natural herb □ known now to be great for medicinal purposes, LOL.

We made up games to play, used old bicycle parts to make new inventions, and played house a lot, LOL □. Occasionally, we got to watch *Fat Albert, Bugs Bunny, The Six Million Dollar Man, The Incredible Hulk,* or *Wonder Woman.* We had one TV in Madea's room. It had pliers attached to the broken knob to aid in changing the channel and aluminum foil on the antenna to get better reception, SMDH □□♂□.

Those were truly the best of days and the worst of days. They were filled with laughter, quickly interrupted by tears of pain from the many whoopins we all got, especially me. I would hear, "The more I talk to you, the worse you get!" Those words often came from my Madea as she squinted at me through her cat-eyed glasses. I was B-A-D, bad! Madea would say, "When I get a hold of ya', I'ma get cha' for the old *and* the new." I've often reflected on my early years, and I know I was challenging, but not because I wanted to be defiant, and not in a disrespectful way. I was mischievous, even destructive. I sought affection, nurturing, and attention in any way I could find it.

I got disciplined nine days a week—with a switch, extension cord, leather belt, or whatever was readily available. Although beatings sound harsh and inhumanc—I gct it—let me tell you what those whoopins did for me. Ultimately, they kept my lil' Black ass alive. They kept me out of jail. Those ass-beatings taught me the importance of saying, "Yes, sir" and "No, ma'am," to my elders. Those whoopins taught me to keep my mouth closed when I wasn't being spoken to. Those whoopins taught me accountability and responsibility. They taught me to honor the sacrifices of my forbearers. Those whoopins taught me wisdom, discipline, and restraint.

Today, many parents and guardians are adamantly opposed to spanking children. The sophisticated folk suggest whoopins are akin to slave beatings. They suggest spanking children breeds violence and aggression. My Madea came from the school of "Spare the rod, spoil the child." While I didn't like that kinda medicine, maybe it saved me from a life of unaccountability, crime, and violence. I am, in large part, the man I am today because of the love my Madea showed me, although I didn't see it like that then. I felt my grandmama didn't like me. She demonstrated no physical affection and didn't verbalize her love for me. Nonetheless, I survived. When I needed Madea, she was there. If I strayed from what I knew to be right, I got in trouble.

Because of Madea's guidance, I only had one brush with the law, and that was more from my own ignorance than from any willful wrongdoing. I thought having checks meant I had money, regardless of what was in my bank account. Not to make excuses, but I'd never been educated or exposed to any level of financial literacy. There was so much I didn't know when I went out into the real world. I had to figure it out, in many instances, at my own peril. I grossly mismanaged a bank account I opened. This would be my first and only brush with the law. My grandmama didn't rescue me. She made me save myself. I learned invaluable lifelong lessons—lessons in integrity, financial literacy, accountability, responsibility, and honor. Through it all, God granted me the strength to delete that "poor ol' me, damaged goods" mentality and adopt a winner's mindset.

I never wanted to be the victim—deep down inside, it was imperative to maintain a victor's perspective.

Chapter Summary

❖ Everything I needed to know in life, I learned in kindergarten: be kind, follow directions, and clean up behind yourself.

❖ Though tough, I seized the good stuff from my childhood. "He who earnestly seeks good finds favor..." (Proverbs 11:27 [New King James Version]).

❖ I chose to make the "main thang" the main thang. The main thing was my survival!

❖ When life throws you lemons, find honey and make lemonade.

In the Middle

When I left Catholic school, I attended Mt. Olive High School. My first year, I fared quite well; my transition was seamless. But, oh, in the third grade, things changed.

The most memorable change was being bullied. Growing up in my Madea's house meant I wasn't allowed to watch any violence or inappropriate content on TV, and the only music played at home was gospel or blues. Our usual TV programs were *Hee-haw, The Lawrence Welk Show, Roots,* or the nightly news. I didn't get to watch *King Kong, Godzilla,* or "that kinda nonsense," as Madea would call it.

One morning, after arriving at school and prior to class starting, several boys gathered in a circle on

37

the playground to talk about the prior night's *King Kong* TV movie series. Since I didn't get to watch the movie, I had no firsthand knowledge. Standing in the circle, each boy took turns recalling their favorite scene. When my turn came, I'd repeat what someone else said before me, LOL □. That happened two or three times.

A boy in the circle named Stanley Cotton, from the brickyard community—a community known to be rough and tough—noticed what I was doing. He got in my face and said, "All you're doin' is just repeatin' what everybody else has said already." Of course, I denied it, and that angered Stanley. Stanley was known to be a bully, and I was scared of him. I *definitely* didn't want to fight him! But he insisted. I fought him out of fear, and, to my surprise, I whooped his ass! From that time forward, I didn't have any more problems with Stanley Cotton. Actually, he tried to be my friend.

Although I thought I'd done a good deed by standing up for myself, I got a good extension cord whoopin' for fighting in school. I couldn't win for losing, SMDH □□♂□!

During my days in elementary and middle school, teachers, nuns, and the principal could paddle you on the butt with a leather strap or board—one with perfectly round holes up and down the middle, so the wind could appropriately pass through the holes and connect succinctly with your behind. Some of my teachers—namely my third-grade teacher, Ms. Gamble—tapped you on knuckles with the metal strip part of a ruler □. None of us liked knuckle paddles, but we loved Ms. Gamble! She was a no-nonsense, mother-like figure who made learning fun.

Unfortunately, I didn't feel that way about all my teachers. I had one teacher, Ms. Ramsey, who was a White lady I truly believe did not care for me. Her energy was horrible, and she was visibly uncomfortable around a class full of Black students. One day, Ms. Ramsey slapped me on my backside with her open palm. Immediately recalling my grandmother's constant fights with White folks about her farm and hunting land, I slapped her ass back!

Of course, I got a whoopin' for the ages. And Ms.

Ramsey held me back in fifth grade. From then on, I learned my lesson and paid attention. I had learned I couldn't control the actions of others, but I could control how I responded—the sage words of my Big Dad. I had so many powerful giants who had poured wisdom into my pitcher of life.

Ms. Alexander, my sixth-grade algebra teacher, was relentless in teaching math. There was no foolishness tolerated in her class—not even a tad bit. When she called on you, you'd better be prepared. If you weren't, you'd meet a wrath unknown to chil'ren anywhere, LOL ☐!

You talk about old school—life didn't get any more "old school" than my experiences. Madea bought or sewed me a few pairs of school pants, and I had a pair of shoes for church and a pair for school. I remember my school shoes—Buddies or Bobos. They were cheap, off-brand, and unfashionable, all white with black or blue stripes. The fastest way to get laughed at during school was wearing Buddies. Due to wear and tear, and it didn't take much wear, the soles of mine would separate from the upper part of the shoe, LOL ☐. I would try to inconspicuously tie them back together, LOL □, but they'd flap anyway, LMBAO □□□.

Kids would jive me to no end...that shit was funny as hell. Imagine an unsightly pair of generic sneakers with a string around the toe...you'd laugh too, LOL □. There was a chant associated with the marketing of Buddies: "Buddies, they make your feet feel fine. Buddies, they cost a dollar ninety-nine." I mean, *damn*, LOL □!

I couldn't deal with those damn Buddies, so to make some money, I developed an entrepreneurial spirit early on. My side hustle in third, fourth, and fifth gradc was sclling snacks. My Madca brought all kinds of cookies and pies home from work. She worked at a snack-making factory called Tom's, along with my Uncle Bull. Madea was an assembly line supervisor. Each day, I waited with bated breath and glistening eyes to see my new inventory. My Madea wasn't aware of my entrepreneurial endeavor, so I had to be stealth in my operations. I took brown grocery bags full of a variety of snacks—moon pies, crackers, cookies, wafers—to school for resale. If the snacks in the school vending machines were twenty-five cents, I sold my snacks for fifteen cents. I was all about a competitive advantage and supply and demand, and I always sold out, LOL ☐.

I enjoyed lots of laughter and fun times in school. But sadly, I also experienced pain and hurt that no kid should ever experience. In fifth grade, at just ten years old, I was compromised, my innocence stolen. The perpetrator was my band teacher, Mr. July. One school day, he told me to go home, get Vaseline, and bring it back to school; I did. The next day, he told me to tell my teacher, Coach Gardner, a fat-bellied, heavily bearded man, that I had to finish work in his class. I believed then, and I believe now, Coach Gardner suspected what was going to happen to me. He had a strange look on his face when I told him Mr. July had told me to come to the band room to learn my trumpet sheet music. I will never forget that look! He was dubious about letting me leave his class to go to the band room and be molested by my band teacher.

I still remember the smell of July's breath and the sexual odor of Vaseline and unadulterated ass. There lay my ten-year-old body, fragile and undeveloped, penetrated and bruised. I went home hurting in so many ways. I felt like I couldn't tell anyone. My uncle was Mr. July's close friend from college, and my Madea had often told me, "What happens in this house, stays in this house." Hurt, pain, physical violations, mental abuse...it stayed in that house. That mindset was just plain wrong. If what happens in your house hurts you, tell somebody! Get help and choose healing. At the time, out of fear, I chose otherwise.

After that incident, I was transferred to another school. Since I'd repeated fifth grade and my three youngest aunts had all graduated from Mt Olive High School, it was time for a fresh start. From Wildman Bottom, I took the long bus ride to my new school. At this new school, I knew no one. And for the first time, my aunts weren't at the same school as me; they'd graduated and moved on. I felt alone and out of place. I rode the bus for nearly an hour each way, and I was just miserable. Nevertheless, over the next three years, I completed middle school between Oliver Middle School and Chavala High School. I was beyond relieved that season was over!

The summer before I was to start high school, my Madea sent me to spend the summer with my momma, Myrtis, and my siblings. That summer was hell. I fought with two of my older sisters often. They terrorized me, and I terrorized them. One even stabbed me in the shoulder with a fork during a fight, LOL □. My two brothers were mostly kind and supportive. However, my oldest brother sleepwalked often and punched and slapped me and our youngest brother during his sleepwalking episodes. He always claimed he was unaware of his actions, hmmm □. Nevertheless, my brothers presented no drama at all.

At the end of the summer, nearing time to start school again, I remember my Madea telling me, "It's time for you to go be with yo' brothas, and sistas, and yo' momma." My Madea was becoming too ill to take care of me, and I couldn't live with her anymore. My heart was broken. All my life, I wanted to live with my momma and my siblings. But now, instead of crying for having to live in the country with my Madea, I cried uncontrollably for having to finally leave her and the farm. Madea reminded me of the sage advice and directions she'd imparted to me over the years, hugged me, told me she loved me, kissed me on the forehead, and sent me on my way. You talk about bittersweet—that seemed more bitter than sweet. After I packed my clothes in the car, Uncle Bud drove me to Columbus, GA, and there I was permanently united with my siblings and momma.

All of those whoopins Madea gave me proved useful when I went to live with my momma. There, we were pretty much left to our own devices. Had it not been for the foundation my Madea laid for me, I would have gone astray, perhaps forever. Madea had raised me in the spirit of the scripture. She knew that if you raise up a child in "the way he should go," he will not depart from it when he is older.

I enrolled myself into Baker High School. The school was within reasonable walking distance from the house in Benning Hills. Baker High School was situated at the intersection of Benning and Victory Drive. Immediately outside the school ground's fence was Baker Village, a public housing project. The kids and the adults from Baker Village were not to be fucked with. I paid attention and kept my distance.

In high school, I worked after school in a drug store in Victory Drive Shopping Center. My supervisor was Ms. Kretchmar, a nice, motherly, redheaded White woman. She really liked me and told me I was going to be somebody one day, and to stay focused and keep the positive energy and enthusiasm I carried.

Although I didn't understand it at the time—I definitely wasn't fully aware—there was something special about me, validated by almost all the wise people I encountered. I was becoming the eagle God ordained me to be. I would fly higher. My time with those who had the character of chickens, pigeons, and crows would be limited. Ms. Kretchmar believed in me, and the words she spoke over me landed powerfully. To this day, I have held on to those words.

By contrast, one morning as I was getting ready for school, my own momma told me I was not gonna be anything. She must have woken up on the wrong side of the bed because she started in on me for no apparent reason, as she had done many times before. As I departed, walking up the street away from the house with tears streaming down my face, those words pierced my soul like a ninja's knife. The pain was so poignant I couldn't breathe. I cried the entire time I walked to school, determined more than ever that I was never going to accept those demonic and defeating words. Through my snot and tears, I decided to change the channel from discouragement to encouragement.

I reflected on a time during a huge family gathering when, being rambunctious and daring, I fell off my uncle's car while he was driving on the red dirt road in Wildman Bottom. I lost my grip and was flung into a ditch. I was scraped and scratched from head to toe. When I returned to my Madea's house, bruised, in excruciating pain, and limping, my momma, having already heard what happened from my cousins, beat me so brutally with a plum switch that the scrapes and scratches became prominent open wounds—she beat me to the white meat—I cried ☐ even more as the pain billowed. As I continued to walk, I reminisced about other interactions with my mom, like hearing her deny I was her child on several occasions. I thought about why I was the only one of her seven children she left in the country to live with my Madea. It seemed the tears were unstoppable. As I approached the school grounds, I managed to gain control of my emotions for the time being, wiped my face, took a deep breath, and went into school as if nothing had ever happened. That day, in those moments, I made up my mind I was going to be somebody!

I was very active in high school. I was in the Junior Reserve Officer Training Corps (JROTC) and involved in student government. As a matter of fact, I was elected vice president of my senior class and president of my high school student government association. I was also quite active in my community as the leader of my community Boys and Girls Club. I was determined to do my level best and stay focused.

My teachers saw my potential and were quite helpful. Most of them were Black, smart, courageous, and passionate. They were giants in my mind—Ms. Effie Jo Reed, Ms. Emma Thomas, Mr.

Richard Sterling, and Ms. B. Pierce. I also had an amazing JROTC instructor, LTC Fluker, and a dynamic literature teacher, Ms. Vivian Johnson. They were great too! They were nothing like that Ms. Ramsey, who I'd had a bout with years earlier. All these teachers were loving and caring. I felt they truly cared about the students, our learning, and our success.

While our White guidance counselor was directing droves of Black students to take the military entrance exam—the Armed Services Vocational Aptitude Battery (ASVAB)—she was providing White students with brochures, scholarship leads, and applications for college opportunities. Although most of the Black students' parents probably couldn't afford to send their children to college, we weren't even given a chance. The teachers I mentioned above reinforced the notion that we could be anything we put our minds to, whether it was in college or the military. My teachers simply had no peer to their level of excellence; they were the best! They advocated for us, they taught us life-long lessons, and they were determined we were going to make it. And I did. I graduated from Baker High School, and the same night, I left Columbus, GA with my then girlfriend, Janice, en route to St. Petersburg, FL.

Chapter Summary

❖ When someone—anyone—hurts you, tell somebody and get help so you can heal.

❖ God created you to be amazing; choose to be royalty.

❖ Stand up to bullies—you'll be surprised. Faith and hope can topple fear.

❖ Material things don't determine character. Humility, integrity, kindness, and consideration are a few things that do.

❖ Investing in other people matters and is inextricably linked to your blessings.

❖ You were created to be an eagle. Don't be distracted by chickens and crows.

❖ Do not listen to naysayers, even if they're family. Don't allow anyone to rent space in your head for free.

❖ You can't control what others do; you can

control how you respond.

❖ This is what has happened. So what? What are you gonna do about it? Don't wallow in your pity. Make the choice to soar like an eagle.

My Religion

There are billions of people who believe their religion is supreme based on *their* understanding. I know, religion can be controversial! But no one can convince me the God I worship and serve will banish the flesh of His flesh to purgatory just because one chooses to believe in and practice a different religion. Since I believe God gave His only begotten son for *all* of our sins, I find it abhorrent that any single religion claims only *their* followers will be saved! So many righteous and sanctimonious, holier-than-thou folk believe they know exactly what God thinks. The scriptures state, "For my thoughts are not your thoughts, nor are your ways my ways,' says the Lord" (Isaiah 55:8 [NKJV]).

Because of slavery and the never-ending

struggles of the Black race, I thought God hated Black people. Prejudiced folk in the earthly realm suggest, based on their narrow understanding of scripture, that God cursed Black people because of Ham's "the father of Black people," sins against Noah. In many ways, the myth seems true, as Black people of many nations and many generations have suffered and continue to suffer from the evils of slavery, trickery, oppression, and servitude. I remain tremendously troubled by this notion. Why did God, since the spirit is omnipotent and omniscient, allow all the different races, skin tones, religions, and creeds, knowing the hurt, pain, division, and death they would cause? I have questions—lots of questions! The reality is, the tale about Ham's son, Canaan, being relegated to slavery or servitude because of his father's sins is just that, a tale.

Growing up, I was taught and practiced the rituals and traditions of Southern Baptist churchgoers. One tradition that stands out is the revival and the "moanin' bench"—one's ticket to salvation, or so I was led to believe. The moanin' bench was a pew where sinners sat, kneeled, and prayed during week-long revivals. To get off the moanin' bench, I pretended I got religion. I shouted off, not truly feeling anything, but tired of sitting there night after night after working on the farm all day □.

There was nothing exciting about revival except the big "to-do" that followed on Sunday afternoon. Me and Madea already went to church several times during the week. I was over it! Church on Sunday started with school for all ages, followed by the Baptist Training Union (BTU), congress meeting, then devotion, culminating with a prolonged worship service that lasted from 10:30 a.m. until 2:30 p.m. It was theatrical—singing, preaching, more singing, announcements and fanfare, and folks shouting uncontrollably—certainly a show to be seen. Then we all went to the "watering hole" to drink "shine," or to Sunday dinner at Madea's house, or both.

The politics of the church were on par with any third-rate local, state, or national government affairs operations. My Madea was the church secretary for a spell. I believe she landed that position because her grandparents built and financed the church. I remember the drama in great detail, including the many church anniversaries where southern cuisine abounded. My aunts and Madea would prepare for days. Everybody had to have some of my Madea's collard greens, cakes, and pies. Egg custard and sweet potato pies were my favorite, LOL □. Often times, I'd hear people who didn't attend our church ask, "What did the preacher preach about?"

During Sunday dinner, I'd hear guests and other family members say "I don't know, but he sho' preached! And Buddy, Christine, and Bull to'c da church up. They had the whole church shoutin'." Seemingly, the worship experience was never about hearing and understanding the *word*, but rather, the theatrics of the moment.

I remember how pretentious the experiences were. They were mostly traditions and rituals. Imagine if God came and offered them a first-class, all expenses paid, trip to heaven—"Children, your spirit is required in heaven tonight!"—most of those so-called "church folk" would make every excuse not to go tonight. I suspect many would most likely reply, "God, please give me until next week, next month, or even next year!" Everybody wants to go to heaven, but nobody wants to die. It seems to me a fruit tree should bear fruit sometimes, though, right □?

Church folk, as I've observed, often speak death and destruction over themselves and their families. Although they quote proverbs and scripture, many still practice speaking negativity into their lives. When asked, "How are you, sista? How are you, brotha?" They respond with, "I'm sick and tired, broke, and burdened down." Or they pretentiously proclaim, "I'm blessed and highly favored," but they go home weak, emotionally detached, and lonely, speaking no favor or supernatural power over their circumstances.

After witnessing that kind of behavior and conduct for years, I decided the kind of negativity brought about by deceit, dishonesty, a limited mindset, and poormouthing may not have started with me, but it would end with me. I chose to set a renewed course for myself and my family. According to scripture, the God I serve said, "But those who wait on the Lord shall renew their strength; they shall mount up with wings like eagles, they shall run and not be weary, they shall walk and not faint" (Isaiah 40:31 [NKJV]). So, as heirs to the throne of a royal priesthood, why are we are held hostage to slavery in its new form—mind manipulation?

Consider King James's translated version of the Bible. Why in the hell would I allow a narrative from a horrific man such as King James, or his translated words, to rule over my life? As with laws today, why wouldn't King James translate the Bible to preserve his strategic interests within his kingdom? Organized religion is not for me. I have begun my journey toward spirituality.

I have experienced many different religious rituals. During my military assignment in Hawaii, I visited a large and prominent church. As I entered the building, I noticed ATM machines placed strategically at the entrance and in the front of the church near the pulpit. The service was okay. Afterward, the pastor's lieutenants told me they'd love to have me join. All I needed to do was complete a biographical data sheet and submit my W2. As we departed, I was like "WTF?" I was so turned off. I'd been a practitioner of ritualistic prayer: unauthentic verbal offerings and not believing what I prayed. But this episode caused my frustration with the greed—with selling hope and salvation—to peak. When I came into my own, I decided I would move away from "religion" and focus on my personal relationship with God. I'd had enough of the philosophies of religious superiority.

I grew up as a Southern Baptist in Alabama. Because of my exposure to the wider world, I adopted a non-denominational perspective. In my humble opinion, I believe religion is divisive. All too often, folk use scripture to lend credence to their own narrative and to prove their point of view. Preachers preach the words of songs somebody else wrote or messages to dig at other people's flaws. I think Sunday mornings are the most segregated time in America—and in the world.

It is not my intent to disrespect one's religious freedom. But I *am* declaring no one's religious freedoms shall be allowed to encroach upon mine. I believe there's good in everything. Nevertheless, based on all I've witnessed, learned, and practiced, the divisive institution of religion became a concept of the past for me. Shortly after enlisting in the U.S. Army, I was asked by the folks making my dog tags, "What is your religious affiliation?"

I replied, "No preference."

More than thirty years later, I still have no

religious affiliation and no preference. I enjoy a very strong spiritual relationship with God, and I believe Jesus is Lord. I also believe in enlightenment and living a life of spiritual purpose. I am a spiritual being making every attempt to *live* in this fleshly body.

Though I have very strong feelings

contrary to organized religion, I still go to church or leverage technology and watch via streaming services.

My church is in my heart, and I carry my spirituality with me in my heart every single day, everywhere I go. I pray daily and often. I pray not for myself but for groups of people—for humanity. I pray for people who may be in court, struggling moms and dads, people dealing with hopeless diagnoses, homelessness, sex crime victims, people facing tough healthcare choices, and some of our elected leaders. I also ask God to pray for me, and I've learned to pray God-sized prayers. For me, it's about spirituality, not religion. I attend church often—whether it's within the four walls of a building, whether I'm leveraging technology, or whether it's in my heart—and I really enjoy it.

We are all divinely connected, no intermediaries required. We are one in the spirit. There are many powerful scriptures that have guided me, including scriptures about God's promises. However, the scriptures below are my favorites.

"And we know that all things work together for the good of them that love God, for them who are called according to *His* purpose" (Romans 8:28 [NKHV]). When I'm going through tough times, I reflect on this scripture.

"For God so loved the world that He gave His one and only Son, that whoever believes in Him should not perish but have eternal life" (John 3:16 [NIV]). I have a tattoo of this scripture. I have modeled my life by giving. I find it so amazing that God gave his only begotten son for us.

"No weapon formed against me shall prosper..." (Isaiah 55:17 [KJV]).

I've held on to these verses; they have helped me move beyond great trials and tribulations. Those scriptures have also guided me and encouraged me to remain steadfast and focused.

Chapter Summary

❖ Consider why you have the religion you have. If you're honest, most likely your religion is inherited.

❖ Challenge yourself to unlearn a few things; make your own wise choices.

❖ Religion can be divisive and oppressive. Many

of us use selective scripture—without proper context and translation—to prove some tactical point of view.

❖ Do you truly believe what you pray? What do you really believe? If you had to prove your faith beyond a reasonable doubt, what would be your proof, your metrics, or your indicators?

❖ Be respectful; arguments are not worth your peace. God needs no defense.

A Letter from Mary

Dear Brother Warren,

I stopped by to encourage your spirit. I know you have a tremendous appetite and thirst for details and understanding. I remember your Madea reminding you of the proverb, "In all things, get an understanding." Well, please allow me to share a period of my journey; consider my perspective.

The spirit of God sent the archangel Gabriel. I was a virgin when he appeared and ordered me to bring forth a child without knowing a man. I was chosen to give birth to the Messiah. That's all Gabriel shared with me—that's it! What he didn't tell me was my fiancé wanted to leave me because he didn't believe I was being truthful about my fidelity, my soon-to-be in-

laws would turn their backs on me and accuse me of being a liar and of being unfaithful, and my precious baby would be born in a smelly manger in a dimly lit barn. I would be on the run for more than two years to protect my baby from King Herod's massacre order, and people would lie, spit on, betray, and be mean to my child. God didn't tell me I would witness my dear boy being brutally beaten and have to watch Him carry His cross to Mt. Calvary, or that I would witness the unimaginable pain of my son's thirst. God didn't tell me I would ultimately watch my precious son be stretched wide, nailed to the cross, pierced in his side, and left there to die.

There was so much I wasn't told, but because I had faith and made a choice to jump, I was going to trust God. I was able to remain in peace. Besides, I had given birth to the Messiah, the Great I Am! When you don't have all the details and understanding you desire, let God be your guide. "Trust in the Lord with all your heart and lean not on your own understanding; in all your ways acknowledge Him and He shall direct your paths" (Proverbs 3:5-6 [NKJV]).

The precious hand of God is upon you, and He finds pleasure in prospering you—you shall be redeemed and restored. Peace be unto you, dear child of the most-high God.

Shalom

A New Dawn

In December 1986, after my delayed entry period, I was invited to wear the cloth of America's Warriors—I was a soldier. I will always be a soldier!

In the words of George L. Sypeck:

"I was that which others did not want to be. I went where others feared to go, and did what others failed to do. I asked nothing from those who gave nothing and reluctantly accepted the thought of eternal loneliness...should I fail. I have seen the face of terror; felt the stinging cold of fear; enjoyed the sweet taste of a moment's love. I have cried, pained, and hoped...but, most of all, I have lived the

times others would say were best forgotten. At least someday, I will be able to say that I am proud of what I was...a soldier."

To whom much is given, much is required. "'For I know the plans I have for you,' declares the Lord, 'plans to prosper you and not to harm you, plans to give you hope and a future'" (Jeremiah 29:11 [NIV].

I attended Basic Training and Advanced Initial Training at Fort Jackson, SC. Afterward, my first assignment took me to South Korea. I was assigned to the Joint Security Area in Panmunjom, Korea. The post was immediately at the border of the Demilitarized Zone. Throughout day and night, North Korean propaganda would play over the loudspeakers. This little Black boy, who had been mostly isolated from the world until then, was more afraid than he'd ever been in his life. My post was the most forward deployed unit on the South Korean Peninsula. Although it was a rigorous and demanding assimilation, once again, I survived.

That assignment was the beginning of my initial

term. My military occupational specialty was legal/administrative assistant. I served from 1986–1989. Then, I was awarded a scholarship and chose to attend Purdue University. I attended Purdue, in West Lafayette, Indiana, for undergraduate studies. This would be my real introduction to White America as an adult. I'd witnessed White people growing up on the farm, as they constantly tried to seize my grandmother's land through manipulation. Whether it was the insurance man or tax collectors, my grandmother constantly fought to keep what was legally hers. I drew from her resilience, but I also inherited her frustrations. From her fight, I learned one must stand for something or fall for anything!

I didn't know anyone in West Lafayette prior to moving there to attend Purdue. I had no idea what was to become of me. West Lafayette is a college town, and at the time I attended, the population was just over thirty-eight thousand students—with only about nine hundred who looked like me. I was scared. I was scared because I'd heard so many stories about the KKK in the region, and I was scared because I thought everybody there was smarter than me. Moreover, I didn't want to lose my scholarship or disappoint the many friends, mentors, and Army leaders who supported me and helped send me there. I quickly learned about the cheating, test sharing, and "coordinating" that went on. I learned no one was better than me, and I wasn't better than anyone else either.

There was little to no diversity, however, it was a very good school. I chose Purdue because I wanted and needed to learn how to adapt to being around others who didn't share my lived experiences. My overall experience was bittersweet and riddled with racial epithets. Less than two years prior to my matriculation, crosses were burned on campus.

I was awarded an Army Reserve Officers Training Corps (ROTC) Green to Gold Scholarship, so I was required to participate in ROTC. I was mostly excited about what was to come as far as my military career was concerned. But to get there, I would have to undergo a rigorous process, not just physically, but also intellectually, emotionally, and mentally. The mental challenge was enduring the rhetoric from military officers asking me why I chose Purdue. They told me I didn't belong there, and I'd be more comfortable somewhere else. Although I made every attempt to dismiss their negativity, their words wore on me. I began to second-guess myself. I even became intimidated by my surroundings.

These men were culturally incompetent and lacked the basic decency every military officer should possess. One man was a short, pudgy Italian who dipped tobacco and often discharged racial epithets. The other was a tall, blond-haired guy who was blatantly biased toward me and the one other Black cadet in the program; he often used dog-whistles to discretely convey his intimidating messages. He was unrepentant and entitled. He had no shame; all the cadets knew he was married as he engaged in an affair with a cadet from my cohort with little to no discretion. Their behavior went unchecked, and the vitriol they spewed was poisonous. I've had great leaders, and I've had poor leaders. I learned a lot from both. They were necessary for me to reach my destiny. However, at Purdue, the two military officers who were my instructors were the worst of the worst.

All the officer cadre were White men, except for the short, pudgy Italian. My saving graces were the Black Sergeant Major, the Black supply sergeants, and, to my surprise, the two White women who worked in the front office. Sometime prior to my last year in Army ROTC, a new professor of military science took the reins. He was the very best example of an outstanding officer. He was a White man who was fair, strong in his faith, loved his family, and showed genuine concern for me. His actions and modeling—positive leadership, integrity, his compassion, and his empathy impacted my life forever. I have very kind memories of him, and he encouraged me to push through and make

the best of all my experiences while attending Purdue. He favored me and often invited me to join him and his Lutheran faith family for church and a Sunday meal.

In addition to my exacting obligations in my commissioning program, I also served in the student senate, as a senior leader in my ROTC battalion, and became a resident assistant in my dormitory, Tarkington Hall. I was not only in charge of students, but also an entire dorm wing, where I supervised four other counselors. That was one of the many sweet parts about attending Purdue. I have no regrets, and I'm glad I chose to delete the negative words of those who'd rather see me fail. My Madea often said to me, "Leave the situation better than you found it."

At Purdue, I believe I left things a lil' better than I found them. I did adapt while maintaining my truth without compromising my identity. I did graduate from Purdue University with a commission in the Army. And most importantly, I got a bold introduction to how White people think and do business. I learned a lot, and not all from books. I engaged White folk in many conversations, as they were sarcastically curious about what they thought they knew about Black people. They asked questions from a perspective that generally reeked of privilege and entitlement and made suggestions implying Black folk needed to pull themselves up by their bootstraps. To their chagrin, they failed to realize leg-up programs like social security (which excluded domestics—Black people), public housing (created for White women who were military spouses), or the GI Bill weren't established and implemented with Black troops in mind. Those who feed from the public trough are usually fine with social welfare as long as the "undesirables" don't benefit.

How quickly folks choose to have selective memories. Oftentimes, Black people are lambasted even though, under dire circumstances, we've still made significant strides in pulling ourselves up by our bootstraps, and we weren't even wearing boots. I believe it is imperative for others, who have benefitted greatly from White privilege, having much of their advancement attributed to the brutal sacrifices of others, consider another perspective. Benefit and privilege, like the land grant that facilitated Purdue University's existence, reparations to Asians, and public aid to White folk are benefits enjoyed with no acknowledgement they were accorded on the backs of those who built an unshakable foundation—foundational liberties and amenities some people so carelessly exploit with little to no reflection on the profound sacrifices of the enslaved. God doesn't allow trials without divine purpose. So, for those of us who have been mistreated, oppressed, suppressed, enslaved, left out, or counted out—get ready. God's unprecedented favor is on the way. He's preparing us for payday! Without fully realizing it, my payday had already started! □□□□

Although I marveled at being promoted to specialist/E4 less than a year after enlisting in the Army, the day I received a commission from the President of the United States as a second lieutenant in the active Army, I was overjoyed, beside myself. I would be privileged to command troops, work alongside them, and serve their families—it was the highlight of my career. I was in amazement over what God had done. I reflected on how I'd triumphed over the many challenges from my early childhood. I remembered and reflected on the many challenges I overcame while studying at Purdue University. One of those reflections was uniformed military officers challenging me as to why I chose Purdue and suggesting I'd be more comfortable at another university. I reflected on my mother telling me, "You ain't gon' be nothin'." I proved them all wrong!

May 14, 1992 was the first day of the rest of my life. I graduated from Purdue and was commissioned as a Field Artillery Officer in the U.S. Army. I wanted to be a combat soldier on the frontline where the action was—or so my bravado made me think. I remained in service through February 2011. In total, I completed more than twenty-four years of service in the Army. I participated in Kosovo as the chief operations officer during the ethnic cleansing debacle between the Serbs and the Croats. I also participated in Bosnia, Afghanistan, and Iraq as a senior staff officer. They were the best of times and the worst of times.

I witnessed a lot of waste of military materiel. The military industrial complex was getting paid! The "*friends*" of the military industrial complex are the biggest public trough feeders anywhere. These corporate welfare recipients take from the "have-nots" to feed the greedy—oops, the "haves." Meanwhile, the "have-nots" continue to have not. But as a distraction, the wealthy highlight Becky's dependency on public assistance. Millions—maybe even billions—in federal contract opportunities are awarded to defense and other contractors with little to no oversight or measured deliverable return. During my time in federal government service, I witnessed a source selection committee select a bidder without competition or protest, based solely on personal relationship. A popular contractor won a generous award to conduct an eight-week strategic assessment. In return, the final deliverable was a 109-page PowerPoint briefing, SMDH 🗛🗛♂🗛. Because they enjoy a reputation and name recognition, they are allowed to get away with little to no accountability; these influencers and good-'ol boys and girls have the "hook-up"! The end users are too afraid to question their products out of fear of reprisal because the contractors wield a lot of power and influence. Consider the national annual budget is approximately six trillion dollars. Given non-discretionary spending/appropriations, like defense and social security, the Pentagon enjoys an annual budget equal to approximately twenty percent of the national budget, excluding supplementals. That's a lot of loot—more than the entire annual budget of many developing countries.

While there were many practices I cringed at during my military service, I thoroughly enjoyed my time serving; there were many more amazing experiences to offset the injustices. I benefitted immensely from extensive travel and exceptional leadership. I am so fortunate to have traveled the globe and enjoyed making new friendships and associations too numerous to recount. I know God had a calling on my life early on, even though I didn't understand it. I had to endure pain so I could gain perspective and become the compassionate servant leader I am today. My life started out rocky, but I would be a "chosen one," who would travel the globe and be exposed to experiences that impacted so many facets of my life.

Fiji was my favorite place, primarily because of its people—authentic, kind, humble, and all around good-natured human beings. They are very happy people. Their spirit and energy are great. They are people of color—Black Polynesians. Although some would suggest they're racist, in my opinion, they are trying to preserve their own culture just as every other culture does in America and around the world. When I say I'm "pro-Black," or "Black lives matter," culturally incompetent people tend to look upon that proclamation with a level of profound scrutiny and prejudicial judgment. Yes, I am interested in preserving the human race. But I am also interested in preserving Black people's culture and history. To measure the truth in the statement "All lives matter," let's consider, on a surface level, the disparities in healthcare, education, taxes, incarceration, homeownership, wealth, transportation, justice, and employment. If all lives truly mattered, why is it that across the tracks, where the underserved and underprivileged Black and Brown folk and the poor White folk live is also the place where the factories are, where the contaminated water is, where the food deserts are, where healthcare disparities are too atrocious for the mind to reconcile? The problem is far greater than the superficial. Traumatic experiences are real across the tracks in communities where people's DNA have long memories and are counted out because of their race and class. I am an extraordinarily passionate servant/leader who has committed my life to the service of others and *doing* my part, above and beyond, to deliver meaningful change!

You see, although I wasn't victorious in my bid for congress, some of the primary reasons I sought a federal elected office was to be a strong and unapologetic advocate for all people, including Black and Brown people. Moreover, to lead causes and efforts aimed at closing the gaps and disparities in neighborhoods below the scratch line; to usher in equality and justice for all. In so doing, I could testify in earnest, "All lives do matter!"

I have so many proud moments working with

certain teams and groups of people, including when I became the first captain in the history of the Army to serve on Capitol Hill in the U.S. Senate. However, my proudest moment was taking troops into combat in Kosovo and Bosnia. Under my leadership, I brought them all home alive.

The military reinforced the things my grandmother instilled in me: character, integrity, loyalty, respect, dignity, honor, grace, mercy, and compassion. I credit the military for a lot of my growth, particularly when it comes to discipline, leadership, and humility. Although many Americans experience tough times, by the world's standards, our problems are simple, particularly when it comes to domestic issues. We at least have access to certain public assistance opportunities. However, when you travel the globe and are exposed to the international standard of living, it is quite humbling. The military reinforced my perspective to be thankful and humble for my citizenship as an American.

In the words of Michele Ruiz, "If people are doubting how far you can go, go so far that you can't hear them anymore."

Chapter Summary

❖ Be grateful in all things, including even the smallest of blessings.

❖ Pain has purpose.

❖ Stand for something or you'll fall for anything.

❖ Be you and be unapologetic about it!

❖ To whom much is given, much is required.

❖ Good and positive leadership is just as important as bad leadership, you need both to excel.

❖ Do good and make every effort to leave every situation better than you found it.

❖ Most every adult is about self-preservation— be bold about yours and your communities'.

Pretending

All the emotions from my younger days—all the physical hurt, all the loneliness and pain—I hid them and refused to ever allow those demons to surface again. I tucked my emotions deep down in my subconscious so I could thrive. I pretended I was strong, emotionless, and happy. In reality, I didn't love myself. I didn't even *like* myself. I could tell by how I treated myself, by all the indicators of compromise, of self-sabotage, and of meager self-esteem. I felt that since my mom didn't love me, why should I love me? Nevertheless, God had a different plan for me!

No matter my afflictions, imperfections, or faults, God looked beyond them all and loved me. He was working behind the scenes for my good. I believe God doesn't restore us to the same state as we were before our challenges—He turns ashes into beauty.

As a Black man, I grew up in a space where men didn't show appropriate levels of love and affection. My family didn't do a lot of hugging, we didn't communicate about our feelings, and we didn't tell one another "I love you." I moved on from that place. I wanted to know love, I wanted to communicate, and I wanted to reconcile my feelings...feelings of disconnectedness and loneliness. There was a void inside me, and I didn't know what to do, who to talk to, or what to say if I *did* speak to someone. Compounding my struggles were remnants of my Southern Baptist roots—religious rituals that dictated, "Just pray, and God will provide." To speak about mental health treatment was to admit you were "crazy" and you should be admitted to the psych ward of the nearest facility. Therefore, I continued to spiral without getting the help I so desperately needed. After the tragedy on September 11, 2001, I attempted to take a step toward what would turn into more than a decade-and-a-half's journey to self-awareness, to no avail. On that tragic September day, I was assigned to monitor local hospitals to account for injured military personnel being admitted. There was so much carnage at the Pentagon. I was on assignment in the Military District of Washington with the Department of the Army's Human Resources Command. I was also going through a legal separation from my wife, which would later become a divorce. I was badly tattered emotionally. It seemed all the emotions and subdued feelings surfaced at once. I had no idea where to even begin confronting my issues; I needed help! I had some serious emotional disconnects. I felt mental health counseling was too taboo in the Black community—frowned upon. The norm was to pray and ask God for deliverance—no therapy necessary. I knew I could pray and ask God for healing from my mental battles. I also believed God ordained and provided professionals to address our emotional and mental instabilities.

Given my history of trauma, and the generational trauma of those who came before me, pretending and hiding was no longer acceptable to me. I knew, as I neared the end of my military service, I had to find a way to put Humpty-Dumpty back together again. I badly wanted a decent chance of assimilating back into the larger society. I started recognizing, more and more, serious symptoms of Post-Traumatic Stress Disorder (PTSD). The weight of all the emotional stress nearly buried me. A lightweight, I drank more, and my youngest daughter seemed sad but pretended to be okay for my sake. Though I was nervous and afraid, my mental health took precedence. One morning, sitting in my bed in a dark, cold room, I made the decision to get help. My fear was real. I considered what others would say, and I considered the impact it would have on my military career. In my experience, Army officers don't *have* problems; they are expected to *solve* the problems of their troops, their families, and their units.

I was also afraid of having to report my treatment during any security clearance updates. I was naked and afraid ☐. I made the call anyway. When a representative of Military One Source answered my call, she could tell I was nervous. She reassured me she was there to help. The first thing I asked her was if my call was going to remain private. Then I requested pairing with a non-military provider because I thought that would help maintain my privacy.

The civilian provider I met with shortly after my initial call for help changed my life! You see, I was spiraling. I cried for no reason, I couldn't sleep, and I was defensive, withdrawn, and emotionally unavailable. My new therapist helped me become willing to be vulnerable and to begin mending the broken pieces. I confronted the pain of abandonment, molestation, rejection, dejection, failure, and discrimination. Over weeks and months, I continued my therapy, and before I knew it, years had passed, and I was becoming a man I didn't even recognize. I was emotionally available, self-aware, wiser, tempered, matured, empathetic, and loving to myself and to others. My deep depression and anxiety and my overall health were taking a turn for the better. I let go of the shame; I took back my power by leaving the labels behind. My new normal was peace.

Without question, my healing rested in my vulnerability. I wrote letters to the predator who violated my innocence, to my momma, and to myself. I apologized to myself for how I'd treated myself and how I'd allowed others to treat me. I never mailed the letters to July and my momma, but the exercises were therapeutic—I survived, and I was never the same again. I was quite deliberate about my engagements with people. Moving forward without missing a beat, my homeboys and I began to share positive emotions. We told each other "I love you" face to face, circumstance permitted.

The sad reality is many Black people have a limited mindset concerning mental health treatment, mostly perpetuated by religion and believing we can't be victorious. Unconsciously, many never stopped seeing themselves as slaves. Mediocrity is permeated throughout communities of poverty. For so long, poor and underprivileged people—many of whom are Black—have been told "*no*", marginalized, and counted out! As a result, many of us have adopted a mindset of lack and defeat, and accept whatever we can get, even the crumbs. The minds are yet shackled—conditioned to believe average and substandard is okay. And we are masters at masking and disguising the pain, trauma, and disappointments, thus leading a very pretentious life. Somehow, some way, we must break the chains □ and unite. I believe the first step is mental health treatment. The first step is healing generational Post Traumatic Slave Disorder (PTSD), not to be confused with "*Stress.*" Although PTSD wasn't a thing in the United States until the 1970s, enslaved Black people—and many others—have experienced immense trauma since the beginning of slavery. When we consider the science of epigenetics, it's quite easy to trace violent traits and characteristics through our DNA—which has tremendous memory—back to the dehumanization of African slaves on ships, plantations, and on the "block." Real brutality is linked directly to systematic oppression, suppression, violence, depression, abuse, dejection, and rejection. My ancestors were systematically pitted against one another. Influenced by skin tone or the brown-paper-bag test, or by the overseer, Black slaves more loyal to a Mas'sah', were shown great leniency and deference. I once heard my Madea say Black sharecroppers refused to support other Black folk because they'd been indoctrinated with the belief that "Mr. Charlie's ice is colder." The remnants of slavery are perpetual and ever-present. Stripped of confidence, dignity, and respect, my people are in mental disrepair, compounded by all the other shit we've endured. I'm reminded of the scripture, "So the last shall be first, and the first last: for many be called, but few chosen" (Matthew 20:16 [KJV]).

Being vulnerable enough to heal is a tremendous challenge for most—especially Black men. My healing began with me naming my pain and telling my story. I learned not everyone deserves to know all parts of my story, or for that matter, any part of my story. Based on my personal experiences and my journey, I know people will exploit a story and use it during times of disagreement to hurt you. In these writings, I demonstrate the courage to tell my entire story. In the words of Maya Angelou, "There's no greater agony than bearing an untold story inside of you."

Chapter Summary

❖ It's cool to profess, as a man, agape love for your fellow man, your brother, your male friend.

❖ God ordained preachers, teachers, and evangelists. He also ordained psychologists and psychiatrists. Do not let anyone hold you back from your restoration, from your healing.

❖ God uses trials to grow our spiritual muscles—no test, no testimony.

❖ Not everyone deserves to know your story; they are just not mature enough.

I Dreamed A Dream

I know God has a calling on my life. I understood early on that my life was bigger than me. I knew I was meant to be a part of something bigger than myself. Spiritually, I felt a deep sense of purpose. Those who God called, he also qualified. Many are called, but few are called again, LOL ☐! Seriously, many are called, but few are chosen.

Many people, most of whom I didn't know, told me I was peculiar. Many respected spiritual leaders proclaimed God's favor upon my life. Others told me I should be a preacher. While flattering, the absolute last thing I wanted was to be a preacher. No how, no way—I am absolutely *not* interested and never even dreamed of being a preacher. My work is in the vineyards, meeting people where they are and helping them get to where they're trying to go. I'm here to speak up for those who don't have the courage to speak for themselves, and to stand for those who are weak. For so long, I've stood in the gap, being the blessing to so many. I finally realized part of my life's purpose is to be the blessing people pray for.

Ten years prior to launching my first political campaign, while serving in Hawaii, I began to write out my plans to seek public office after my retirement from the Army. I wrote out my dreams and plans so I could visualize them. I'd been taught if you write down your dreams or make a vision board, the chance of them coming to pass is significantly increased. I carried and nurtured this God-ordained dream almost all my life. As a child, I remember proclaiming that I would be a soldier, a great dad, and President of the United States (POTUS). As I aged and became more enlightened, I refined my prayers about becoming the POTUS. I decided to become an outstanding elected official. It was there in Hawaii, in 2005, that I asked God to allow me to be a U.S. Congressman. I had no reason to believe God wouldn't once again grant the desires of my heart. As I looked back over my life, even though there were trials and tribulations, God had pretty much allowed me to succeed in every endeavor I'd embarked upon.

However, once I got to the point of campaigning, I realized I was too naïve for this cutthroat endeavor. I enjoyed the generosity, selfless service, and the downright hard work of several faithful, dedicated, and loyal campaign staff, all of whom were volunteers. They were truly "ride-or-die for Warren." I shall forever be grateful to them for their unwavering support. However, most of the so-called "paid political operatives" were looking for a check. I allowed far too many feckless and mendacious people to occupy my space. They promised a lot and delivered little or nothing at all. So many self-absorbed folks refused to be held accountable. I recall asking the question "What am I getting for the money I'm paying for this service? What are the metrics of success?" You would've thought I'd asked these moochers for their firstborn child. They became very defensive and puzzled because I'd asked such questions. When I realized what was happening (while I was overwhelmed with just being a candidate), I was in trouble. I'd spent hundreds of thousands of dollars—my life savings—and had little to show for it. Moreover, I wasn't a favorite of the "establishment," as most didn't have the intestinal fortitude to take a stand when they knew the incumbent was not serving the district well. I wrote checks in support of political incumbents in the county/congressional district, with promises of support offered in return. These cowards would declare, "I'm a fan, Warren," but lacked the courage to *do* anything.

A very astute and kind White gentleman in Arnold, Maryland, told me he would only vote for me if I could explain, with a good level of detail, what I was going to do to help my own people—Black people. He explained how other races owned and controlled institutions and industries like banking, the judiciary, the financial markets, media, defense, education, commerce, political institutions, housing, and healthcare. An hour after I knocked on his door, we were happily engaged in conversation. He shared, I shared. I left with the promise of his vote and a very generous campaign contribution. I felt more enlightened and more courageous. I reflected on everything we'd talked about and concluded he was right—Black people don't own or control any industry or institution in America. We *could*, but division, fear, and apathy dominate our collective existence. We're extremely talented. However, we often sell our intellectual properties for pennies, whether it be in the entertainment, sports, or food industries. Rarely, if ever, have I heard Hispanics, Asians, Jews, or any other ethnic group apologize for being staunch advocates for their communities and their interests. But Black folk often get pushback when it comes to standing up for our communities. People cite fairness and other righteous bullshit when we advocate for other Black folk. We're always apologizing for being Black—damn!

I met so many people who believed in me and my heartfelt message, and they supported me in words and in deed. People often told me they saw my heart and knew I was sincere about service. My work ethic was unmatched. My ground game had no peer. But it took a lot more than a tactical ground game. I didn't have the $1.5–$2 million it would take to win a congressional race. Figuratively speaking, I had jumped into the Pacific Ocean. Although I was a very strong □□ swimmer, I didn't have a life vest, the temperature was way too cold, and the waves □ and undercurrent were too strong, so I drowned □. Nevertheless, God rescued me again □□□□□.

Voters knew many of the politicians in the county were feckless and bloviated, that they were passive and lacked courage and vision. But the electorate is not well engaged or informed. The level of political complacency is exploited; people who are "super voters" (they vote most of the time in all elections), courted via mailers, go to the polls, and vote for the name they know, not having any real tangible or measurable expectations. Though I am beyond grateful for all the work past and present legislators at all levels have done to help get us to this point, I strongly believe that for many, it's time to take a knee. Rarely do we groom the next generation of elected officials...many stay until death. I am an avid supporter of term limits at every level of elected office.

The alternative is that "our" elected officials become bought and paid for by special interest groups. I have witnessed local politicians who sold their votes be subject to public ridicule and denigration. As sad as it is, many politicians are woefully ignorant and willing to do whatever it takes to maintain their seat, or more accurately, the seat of the *people*. In my heart, I believe Black legislative power is selling Black folk back into slavery. It's sad. According to *Sludge Report*, "In a lobbying contribution report filed with the House of Representatives, CoreCivic, (a private prison conglomerate, with detention centers all across America), disclosed donating $25,000 in "honorary expenses" to the CBC-linked Congressional Black Caucus Institute (CBCI) on April 15, 2019. CoreCivic made a similar donation of $25,000 to CBCI in 2018."[1]

When lobbyists make such donations, they

---

[1] https://prospect.org/civil-rights/congressional-black-caucus-institute-takes-corecivic-cash-boosts-policies-help-private-prisons/

expect their special interests to be represented and addressed through policy and through legislation. They're expecting advocacy and, in this case, they are expecting beds to be filled—by Black men and women from districts CBC members represent.

Black folk often speak of "poor White trash" (PWT) people voting against their own best interests. However, many of us, several of whom are well-to-do, vote against our own interests as well. We often vote for politicians who provide poor constituent services. Their legislative votes are bought and paid for by special interests, and they bring no groceries (tax dollars or economic development projects) back to their communities, SMDH □□♂□. Thus, they deliver constituent-based legislative victories quite sparingly, if at all. But, with the assimilationist mindset, so many embrace "go along to get along" perspectives.

Black people are expected to accommodate others' sensitivities. However, Black folk's sensitivities are rarely validated by institutions and centers of power. Often, Black people are expected to forget the trespasses or sins of the father because

"It wasn't *me* who oppressed you," (a debate to be hashed out at a later time and date, LOL ▢), and move on. Are the Japanese expected to forget internment camps? Are Jewish people expected to forget Auschwitz? Of course not! So why in the hell do Black people allow others to even utter such a ridiculously stupid and suppressive statement? I will never forget, and I will never allow anyone to even suggest that I *should* forget! SMDH ▢▢♂▢. Should anyone stereotype a Jew, they are going to face a litany of fiery consequences. You stereotype a Black person, it's just okay—acceptable. Many Black people allow other races to treat them poorly. Black folk cannot own real estate in places like China and in some other countries. However, people of any other land, especially Asia, can own whatever they choose and can afford in America. The circumstances beg the question, "Who's advocating for us—Black people?" I often ask myself, why aren't Black legislators fighting to keep Black college athletes from being sold—their intellectual property and their talents being seized for the economic advancement of institutions that would otherwise dismiss them? Why aren't they fighting to keep land from being stolen from Black landowners? Why aren't Black legislators doing their part collectively to ensure the next generation of flag officers are enrolled in the military academies?

We must demand a full plate and a seat at the table and stop settling and being content with mere crumbs—in education, criminal justice, prime government contracts, politics, healthcare, homeownership, and SBA low interest loans—by any means necessary. America has never conquered anything without a battle—a fight. However, when Black people fight for their rights, for equality, and for liberty and justice for our people, we're labeled and castigated as anarchists, SMDH □□♂□□□

Black people submit themselves freely to White folk even in the face of the most egregious infractions. However, we will literally eat another Black person alive for the simplest of violations against us. No matter what, people will always see Black people as just that: Black—almost not human. As a society, we are very accustomed to labels and boxes because we can process people's perceived worth better that way. I've had so many friends say to me, "Warren, when I see you, I don't see color." I think, □ *that's bullshit!* To not see color is to not see *me.* What if I said to a woman, "When I see you, I don't see gender"? That would invoke outrage, and it should. Please, don't let anyone tell you they don't see you! Where is your courage?

As Malcom X said, "...tomorrow belongs to the people who prepare for it today." My ancestors laid a tremendous foundation, and I shall not allow their sacrifices to be in vain. They died heinous deaths believing in but not realizing freedom, equality, and justice. Many died without witnessing and experiencing the service of our first Black president of the USA. Please don't be tricked. Pay attention to the messages, especially the ones that aren't spoken out loud or nestled in code.

President Barack H. Obama, the most erudite, honorable, and tempered chief executive our country ever had, experienced disrespect on levels baffling to the mind. When a White man declared, "It's my mission to ensure he's a one-term president," or when a politician called him a liar during a State of the Union Address, the strategic massage was clear. While the words were directed toward the POTUS, the message was for every Black man aspiring to seek the presidency in the future. The way I interpreted the message was "Boy, don't you dare think about seeking this office. You see what we're doing to Barack. It'll be worse for you." On that day, when President Obama was first inaugurated, filled with a pride I'd never known, I declared, "I am not afraid." Wherever my destiny leads me, I shall endure, I shall be courageous and brave, and I shall not be moved! I ain't giving up, I'mma go wherever I gotta go, do what I gotta do, be what I gotta be to honor the sacrifices and preserve the dreams of my ancestors. I had learned being bold and confident yields much fruit. In American culture, the squeaky wheel gets the grease. Therefore, I will not wait or be silent—I operate henceforth in the fierce urgency of now!

"Twenty years from now, you will be more disappointed by the things you didn't do than by the things you did. So, throw off the bowlines. Sail away from the safe harbor. Catch the trade winds in your sails. Explore. Dream. Discover" (Mark Twain).

Inspired by the victory of President Obama, I was fired up and ready to go! Though I'd given everything I knew to give during my own political campaign, for the first time, I lost □□. All of my passion, enthusiasm, my desire to lead and deliver meaningful change seemed all for naught. I felt God had forgotten about me. I thought God had abandoned me. I was lost—bent, cracked, even broken in some places—but not shattered. I buried myself in sorrow, and maybe even a bit of unwarranted shame and pity. I secluded myself and completely abandoned relationships that had only taken away from my joy—the relationships and acquaintances who added no value. I declared a revival over my life—spiritually, emotionally, physically, financially, and psychologically. As I began to reflect, I quickly realized it wasn't my time! I had people around me who weren't supposed to go where God was leading me. I needed to become the energy I desired to attract. This quote from Jim Rohn sums it up: "You are the average of the five people you spend the most time with. The people you spend the most time with shape who you are. They determine what conversations dominate your attention."

I separated myself from a lot of folk—the takers. If you never get away from the wrong folk, do not expect to get to the right folk! Once the takers use you up, they move to the next victim. Can one expect to soar like an eagle □ when one hangs out with chickens? I was reminded that my life in five years would resemble that of my friends. If you walk with wise people, you will become wise. Spirits are transferrable. If the people you spend the most time with are not helping to make you better—adding intangible value, helping to make you smarter, making you laugh, sharing love, helping you become more self-aware, helping to advance your purpose, and moving you closer to your destiny—find new people to spend time with. Birds □ of a feather flock together; iron sharpens iron.

"Surround yourself with the dreamers and the doers, the believers and thinkers, but most of all, surround yourself with those who see the greatness within you, even when you don't see it yourself"

(Edmund Lee).

Regrettably, on more than one occasion, I ignored my intuition. But takers and negative-spirited people were a part of God's plan for my growth. I could have avoided a few tough lessons that almost brought me to my knees. But I'm still standing.

After a short season of weeping and feeling sorry for myself, I embraced the defeat in my political campaign efforts after a very close friend—let's call her Dee—told me, "You didn't lose, you learned." I prayed feverishly for understanding, healing, and restoration. During my season of travail, my doubt, my attitude, and my energy almost shattered everything God intended for me. It wasn't that God said no; He told me "Not right now. It's not your time." After deep reflection, I understood. I learned God will not allow anything to take us out of our God-given destiny. I had a dream which I felt was God-sanctioned. I went through some disappointments and setbacks. Things didn't turn out the way I'd hoped and prayed for. But here's the key: I learned that when one dream dies, you just need to dream another bigger, bolder dream. Just because it didn't work out the way I had it planned doesn't mean God doesn't have another plan for me. I decided I could not allow one disappointment, or even a series of disappointments, to convince me my dream was over. I dug in, prepared for battle, and held on to the promises God planted in my heart.

Chapter Summary

❖ Dream big.

❖ If at first you don't succeed, try and try again.

❖ No matter how many times you fall, get back up and try again—get your no's out of the way so you can get to your yeses.

❖ To see me is to see all of me, including my blackness.

❖ Stay woke—hold people accountable, especially those you are paying to work for you.

❖ Boxes are for shoes, hats, and other "stuff"— not people. Don't allow anyone to put you in a box; you're far too dynamic.

❖ Watch who you keep company with. Birds of a

feather flock together.

❖ Consider another perspective; the ones you have may be toxic.

❖ The oppressor will relinquish nothing without a demand—teach people how to treat you.

❖ Be amazing in your "waiting period"—whatever you do, do it to the best of your abilities.

❖ Pay attention to what people *do*, not so much to what they say. Time is the best teacher.

❖ Your ancestors sacrificed a lot for your current circumstances; don't let their living be in vain. Adopt a rcncwcd mindset.

❖ Honor those who paved the way; forgive but never forget.

A Letter from King David

Warren,

Peace be unto you; I come in peace and love. God started a great work in you, and He's continuing an even greater work in you—He has a supernatural calling on your life. Your greatest challenge is to forgive yourself for past mistakes. Stop replaying your poor choices in your head.

Look to the hills for help. An amazing destiny is assigned to you and your children—believe! God has created your dreams.

Henceforth, speak life over your destiny, to your heart's desires, and delete every thought about what you don't want. To thine own self be true.

God closed doors to get you to the fullness of your

calling. I know you've been disappointed because of all the times you've heard, "No, not yet." You're on the launch pad; awesomeness is in your future. All things work together for the good of those who love God and who are called according to his purpose.

I greet you, brother, in the mighty and magnificent name of our most wonderful Lord, our God. This is King David. I hit you up in your DM on IG; take a look at the message. I know you're busy, so here's the crux of my message. My journey was defined by courage, humility, loyalty, steadfastness, dishonor, leadership, and service. I would be remiss if I left out the notion of the great challenge. You see, I was a scrawny little shepherd boy charged with tending to my father's sheep. I was known to be a faithful servant after God's own heart. When the prophet Samuel showed up at my dad, Jesse's, house to anoint the next king of Israel, I was out tending to my dad's sheep. Samuel met all of my brothers, who were strapping and possessed what most would call king-like stature. My dad dismissed me and relegated me to tending sheep—he didn't think I would amount to much. But Samuel told my dad that none of my brothers were God's choice. Samuel asked my dad if he had another son. The prophet Samuel summoned me from the fields. Immediately, he proclaimed I was the chosen one and anointed me to be the next king of Israel.

I would not be crowned king until thirteen years later. During this time, my dad had me take food to my brothers in battle. This small task seemed minuscule; after all, I'd been ordained to be king. But because of my faithfulness in the small things, I had my bout with Goliath—I slayed him and gained the favor of the current king.

Overnight, I was thrust into royalty. Though I'd gained favor with King Saul, his jealousy caused him to attempt to kill me. I did some treacherous things, like impregnating my best trooper's wife, then sending him to the frontlines of battle where I knew he'd be killed. Nevertheless, God showed me tremendous mercy and forgave me. I also forgave myself.

As you move into your calling—your destiny—trust that God is working behind the scenes for your good. When you feel your time is taking too long to come, remember my thirteen-year waiting period. God finds *pleasure in prospering you. Let God be who he is to you—Jehovah Jireh, "the lord will provide," El Shaddai, "God almighty," and "The Great I am." Peace be unto you, my brother.*

A New Thing

God's spirit—my inner captain—spoke to my spirit, sending the vibes of the words "God is going to blow your mind—he's doing a new thing!" A friend named Akira said to me, "In this season, you are to travel alone during this stretch of your journey." Initially, I was pissed off by her prophecy, and I didn't understand. The last thing I wanted, or thought I needed, was more alone time. But after much prayer and pondering, the message became clear. That alone time was very necessary. It was time I needed to fall in love with me.

Although I was keenly focused on my emotional intelligence, I badly wanted to have distractions because the time seemed void of the intellectual stimulation I'd routinely been a part of in my professional and volunteer service prior to my unsuccessful bid for congress. I very much wanted the dignity associated with meaningful and professional work. Nevertheless, interview after interview, I thought I'd represented myself in outstanding fashion, but ultimately, I wasn't selected. I wasn't naïve; in my experience, who you know gets you in the door, and what you know keeps you in the door. But what I was once great at yielded no favorable results.

Oftentimes, I felt I was more competent in the areas I was being evaluated in than the panel members who were doing the evaluating. Again, I thought God had forgotten about me.

I tried everything...especially leaning on my faith! I professed, declared, and proclaimed greatness. I spoke things even though they hadn't yet come about. For inspiration, I watched *The Secret* over and over and listened to sermons religiously. I attended church and helped people, often using my own meager resources to help them reach their own destiny. Yet, nothing happened! No movement occurred. I couldn't find work commensurate to my education, training, or years of relevant experience. Too many times to count, doors closed. I must have applied for more than two thousand job opportunities commensurate with my skills and abilities. I thought I was getting behind. Time was not on my side, and I was getting too old for a multigenerational workforce. Every time I looked on LinkedIn, I read about my peers—and in some cases, people who once trailed behind me professionally—advancing to new and impressive levels of accomplishment. But even though I saw no visible changes after trying everything I knew, I still believed God was working behind the scenes for my good.

"You are never too old to set another goal or to dream a new dream" (C.S. Lewis).

I was on unemployment benefits twice. When I did gain employment, it was as a substitute teacher. I hated it! I felt irrelevant. I possessed extraordinarily marketable skills but was relegated to being a substitute teacher in a system more challenging than when I wore the uniform of America's greatest warriors. Even in that space, I was treated as if I was incompetent or didn't measure up.

I worked with teachers who looked down on me. I worked with kids who had challenges far beyond any experience I'd had, and I witnessed parenting behaviors that were reprehensible and should have been illegal. Many teachers tried diligently to effectuate meaningful change, but administrators seemed completely overwhelmed, inept, and entitled. They felt, because they'd had some training and read some research, they had all the answers to knowing how to raise and educate our Black children. Many were completely incompetent in the areas of culture and trauma-informed care.

I worked at many schools, and on three occasions, I took long-term assignments. If I'd chosen to, I could have worked every day. I chose not to because it was overwhelming and exhausting. I had served in the U.S. Army for nearly twenty-five years. But working in schools to help educate our children was more challenging than any day in uniform—including my time in combat!

I did the work, but I didn't like it at all. I had no

passion or enthusiasm for the work, and I was unfulfilled. Although I knew a lot, my students didn't care how much I knew until they knew how much I cared. It was important to me to know them by their name, so I made it a priority to learn their names as soon as possible. The single most important thing was engaging with students who, in many cases, *desired* success. I discovered early on that students absorb information in a myriad of ways. If I was going to reach them, I had to figure out how to teach them in the way they learned instead of expecting them to learn the way I teach. Their environments in and out of school just didn't facilitate their desires being met, especially for Black boys. They were nagged at home, then came to school to be nagged some more.

I worked in urban public charter schools, which are dominated by entitled and guilt-conscious White women. The very boys they enable are the same men they will be afraid of in ten to fifteen years. When encountering them on the streets, they'll clutch their purse and their pearls and cross the street to avoid these boys—truly shameful, SMDH □□♂□. It's called White guilt—guilt that enables poor conduct and behavior. The justification is that "they experience so much trauma at home." That may be true but enabling them won't enhance their circumstances. The best solution, in my opinion, is to get them the mental health and psychological treatment they need. In my opinion, their actions must be about their own personal reconciliation.

Many students desperately need mental health and occupational therapy resources in schools, and teachers and administrators know it. But because the system is overwhelmed, funds don't exist, parents are in denial, and students are undiagnosed, the challenges are ubiquitous. The future of these extremely challenged children seems hopeless. Each year, tests scores are reviewed, research is touted, and discussions are held about the same issues—Black boys and how to reach them. Imagine, White women acting as if they can empathize with the homelife and traumatic experiences of a Black boy! Really?

I continued this work for three years. There were days I went home only to try to find some solace in drinking more than usual. I prayed every day for God to deliver me from this assignment. To my ears, the heavens were silent. While I was praying for blessings, I realized God was using me to be a blessing to others. Working as a teacher was never about the money—never! I have never been fascinated with money, and even today, money just doesn't motivate me. When I have an abundance of money, I usually find ways to give it away. I spent most of my earnings from teaching to buy school materials and snacks for the children.

To create a competitive advantage, I retooled and enhanced my skill sets; I went back to school and earned an MBA for executives. I also received certificates in life coaching and project management to make myself more marketable. Still nothing. God spoke to my heart, "I see you; your spiritual muscles are growing—remain steadfast and unmovable. Suddenly, in an instant, your circumstances will change. Your time, your due season, is on the way." I recall thanking God for protecting me from myself, because I wanted to self-sabotage. I wanted to believe what I *saw* instead of God's promises. I found the courage to trust in God and not believe my weary eyes.

God used me to bless others when I felt *I* needed a blessing, a healing for myself. In a season where I felt depleted and needed encouragement, I was pouring mightily into the pitchers of others. I couldn't give up or feel sorry for myself, because I was responsible for setting an example for my daughters, who I love more than life itself. I wanted so badly to break any curses that followed me and change the course of a family legacy that didn't dream like I did. I recalled the lineage of biblical families...who begat whom, and how lineage impacted success. I sought success in hopes of changing the course of the future, so my daughters might enjoy less struggle and a greater degree of success as a result of my sacrifice and hard work. I believed their fate was directly and inextricably linked to the meaning of life their ancestors created. I thought my heredity—my lineage—was forever linked to God's portion...God's promises for my life. Not so! God's favor is not fair and for many, doesn't seem real.

I didn't want my daughters to experience average, mediocre, or common—the story of my lineage. I wanted so much more for them and theirs! I gained tremendous perspective. I chose to focus on all the blessings I *did* have, and not give energy to what I *didn't* have. Though I felt people would judge me because I didn't fit into their definition of success, I made a choice to not seek validation from people who didn't control my blessings. I leaned on a powerful quote from Eleanor Roosevelt: "No one can make you feel inferior without your consent."

The hard drive of my mind was infected—it was hacked by negativity, defeat, dishonor, deceit, and self-sabotage—and withdrawal ran rampant. I implored myself to reformat, disinfect, restore, and reboot a renewed mind to the original settings, where love, peace, joy, kindness, forgiveness, and spirituality reigned. I recalled what God called me— blessed, brave, king, amazing, poised, pedigreed, distinguished, honorable, royal, victorious, *loved,* eagle. God calls me an overcomer. He calls me enough!

I began to stir up those God-given dreams and

saw God pour out His favor and blessing upon me once again! I set my mind on victory, I changed the channel to power, and I reprogrammed my heart to expect my dreams to come to pass. Life is like a puzzle; each piece comes together as we discover a match.

According to the scriptures, "As iron sharpens iron, so one person sharpens another" (Proverbs 27:17 [NIV]).

God shook my tree, and the dead branches fell. God pruned the remaining branches, and they began to bear even more fruit. I didn't like being on the potter's wheel, but I was so gratful for God's mercy and grace, and that He protected me from myself. My trials weren't designed to keep me from my purpose; the tests and tribulations were *preparing* me for my purpose, according to God's measure for me. His assignment for others had little to do with me, other than the paths on which He ordered our steps to cross. I challenged my thoughts and considered an alternative perspective: the perspective of the big bad wolf □ rather than the story of the three little pigs. Often, Black folk—

especially Black men and boys—are cast as the big bad wolf SMDH □□♂□. For perspective, consider the story of *The Three Little Pigs*. Imagine the pigs teasing and antagonizing the wolf. We have only ever read the little pigs' perspective. What if they were throwing rocks and hiding their hands? What if they were daring the wolf, taunting him, and selling wolf □ tickets □? What if they lied, thus falsely accusing the wolf? There have been far too many false allegations made against Black folk, especially Black men. Many of those falsehoods literally cost people their lives. However, privilege and fragile White people refuse to acknowledge that hateful and sinful past. If you deny or refuse to see serious racial disparities, it's ignorance by choice.

"A man convinced against his will is of the same opinion still" (Author Unknown).

All our lives, we've been taught and have adopted other people's perspectives. I dared myself to have the courage to think for myself, to have the courage to unlearn a few things, and to have the courage to truly think outside the box.

My experiences, through time, taught me people

will treat you exactly how you teach them to treat you. I fully adopted Maya Angelou's philosophy, "When a person shows you who they are, believe them the first time." Trust they will show you; time is the best teacher. I learned how to treat myself, how to love myself, and how to teach *others* how to treat me. In so doing, it didn't require indignation. It required courage. I didn't realize the frustration I'd cause for others in demanding a different approach. Honestly, I didn't care how frustrated people would be. Preserving my dignity and my peace was of the utmost importance. I used to always find ways to say yes. But life taught me an important lesson and literally forced me to adopt the philosophy that no means no—the word "no" alone is a complete sentence and deserves no explanation.

It took me a while to fully embrace this new approach. I leaned heavily on my renewed faith. Life seemed much simpler prior to me embracing my spirituality and choosing to believe and trust in God. My peace evaded me. When I declared or decreed goodness over my life, like Job, I wondered where God was. I couldn't hear Him, I couldn't see

Him, but I could feel His comfort. I was constantly tested, but I was also growing spiritually. I tasted peace that surpassed all understanding, and my spiritual growth was exponential.

Chapter Summary

❖ Recognize your own bullshit so you prevent others from having power over you.

❖ You are truly never too old; age is relative!

❖ Hear what God calls you—drown out the white noise.

❖ You are everything God intended—you are enough. If the spirit intended you to be something different, you would be.

❖ Take advantage of every opportunity to retool and remain relevant.

❖ You teach people how to treat you—they will treat you exactly how you teach them.

❖ For part of your journey, you may have to travel alone.

❖ Demand a seat at the table. Please don't settle for crumbs.

❖ There is a season for everything; one thing is

constant—change.

❖ No one can make you feel inferior unless you give them permission. God uses trials to grow our spiritual muscles—no test, no testimony.

❖ I am what I am—a man—a spiritual being trying to soar in this fleshly body and carnal mind.

Gratitude

A few years ago, I chose to focus on the many blessings God has adorned me with. The three life events I'm most grateful to God for are:

❖ Allowing me to be rescued from the pain and heartbreak of my early childhood.
❖ Becoming a dad to my amazing daughters.
❖ Serving in the U.S. Army as a soldier; being a part of something far greater than myself and achieving a sense of belonging.

It is quite easy to complain about what we don't have. However, when we think about all the many things we *do* have, there's a lot to be grateful for. Over the last few years, each night, I've written down an expanded list of the many other things I'm grateful for: my relationship with God, Jesus, spirituality, my daughters and their protection, God's supernatural and unprecedented favor, courage, abundance, my health, my senses, my abilities, love, grace, mercy, dignity, discernment, honor, integrity, wisdom, peace, kindness, joy, humility, respect, forgiveness, faith, salvation, paying off my bills and the bills of others, my benefits and retirement, faithful and meaningful relationships, my positive mindset, food and nourishment, water, my home, my possessions, writing books, restoration, overflow, unprecedented increase, sharing, willingness to be helpful, being debt free, traveling, mercies, understanding, clarity, being a C-suite executive, intelligence, self-awareness, being a dynamic coach and mentor, humanity, willingness to be appropriately vulnerable, serving, strength, movement, God working behind the scenes for my good, healing, empathy, compassion, family, opportunities, financial abundance, hope, healthcare, exposure, God's anointing, good character, rest and sleep, cleanliness, networks and influencers, intimacy, sacrifice, promotion, being mentally healthy, being emotionally available, ability to learn, my sharp memory, my blackness, attitude of gratitude, public speaking, discipline, healthy eating habits, fulfillment, access, patience, the fear of God, and decency.

My list is not comprehensive, but it's a reminder to me of all the things, big and small, God has blessed and continues to bless me with. It provides me with perspective. When I think about not having the shoes I desire, I'm reminded some people have no feet. Some of the declarations I've made have not yet come to pass. I know the energy I put out will be returned to me. I am speaking of things as though they already are. I learned to pray God-sized prayers and not limit my requests to the "May I have twenty dollars?" size. Instead of wishing for just enough cash to get by for another day, I began to pray to pay off my house and the houses of others. That shift allowed me to get out of the boat and walk on the water of faith toward my destiny.

There were those who counted me out, some

military officers who lacked integrity and decency, pitiful civilian leaders, and crafty people who thought they were pushing me down. Little did they know they were pushing me closer to my destiny— I'm grateful to them!

According to the measure and the authority God ordained for me, I was able to speak power, goodness, and life over God's people, and I was able to be an amazing dad, friend, and professional. In my prayers, I began to ask, believe, and receive. I prayed for what I really wanted, what my heart really desired, what brought me joy, and what fulfilled me. Below is a snippet of my prayers:

❖ I am so happy and grateful my daughters are prosperous, victorious, successful, safe, and filled with the spirit of God.

❖ I am so happy, peaceful, joyful, and fulfilled now I am whole by the grace, mercy, and joy of the Lord, my God.

❖ I am so happy, peaceful, joyful, and fulfilled now I am in complete relationship with God almighty.

❖ I am so happy, peaceful, joyful, and fulfilled now I am the owner of a luxury condo of 4,000 square feet.

❖ I am so happy, peaceful, joyful, and fulfilled now I am a multimillionaire.

❖ I am so happy, peaceful, joyful, and fulfilled now my body is fully restored, healthy, and youthful.

❖ I am so happy, peaceful, joyful, and fulfilled now I am about to buy homes for loved ones and the most vulnerable/needy.

❖ I am so happy, peaceful, joyful, and fulfilled now I am an executive doctoral degree recipient in Business Administration.

❖ I am so happy, peaceful, joyful, and fulfilled now I have changed my thinking, my love-filled heart.

❖ I am so happy, peaceful, joyful, and fulfilled now I am in a healthy, respectful, joyous, intimate, and passionate relationship.

❖ I am loving, kind, generous, confident, and intelligent.

❖ I am soaring like an eagle.

❖ I am a bestselling author.

❖ What I really want is to be a federally elected official or political appointee.

❖ What I really want is to travel the world safely and with all the resources I require to live a prosperous and luxurious lifestyle.

❖ What I really want is peace, joy, and love.

❖ What I really want is another career as a senior executive/C-suite leader.

❖ What I really want is to publish my *NYT* best-selling books.

❖ What I really want are multimillion-dollar asscts, including an abundancc of rcsourccs in the bank.

❖ What I really want is to help others fulfill their passions. I want to courageously lead people to greatness.

❖ What I really want is a healthy body and to live with authentic, God-sourced love.

A Letter from Job

Dear Warren,

I have watched you, and wow, am I impressed! Although our tests have been different, the fundamentals are quite similar. I suspect our testimonies will be familiar. You know my story. I've come through to let you know God is watching, he sees you, and he understands. He shall provide; he will never leave you or forsake you—just believe. I know you get frustrated. I know you sometimes wonder where God is and feel God's favor seems unfair. But His mercy and grace are sufficient.

As you know, I was going about my business, not knowing the devil was negotiating for my peace, for my life. Perhaps, for a moment, I felt entitled—this wasn't supposed to happen to me. I was an upright servant of God.

Nevertheless, in the course of one day, I lost everything—my livestock, my servants, my ten children, including daughters who were more beautiful than life itself. The dire circumstances shook me to my core. In my mourning, I still blessed God. And that wasn't enough; Satan ☐ wanted me dead. My body was afflicted from the crown of my head to the soles of my feet. I still blessed God.

As if I didn't have enough to deal with, my wife suggested I curse God and die; I rebuked her in the strongest terms possible and proclaimed, "Though he slay me, yet will I trust in him: but I will maintain mine own ways before him." (Job 13:15 [KJV]). My friends, neighbors, and my critics turned their backs on me and suggested I must have committed evil to offend God. I was in a space where I wished I had never been born. I asked, "Where are you, God?" My circumstances became too much for me to bear. I was angry ☐. I became bitter, sarcastic, impatient, and afraid. My eyes were dim from weeping.

Over a period of what I thought were futile and worrisome months of a horrible affliction *unbeknownst to me, God was watching over me. Because I stood, because I didn't give up, because I praised God in the valley, because I persisted in pursuing good, God gave me beauty for ashes. My measure was restored seven-fold, and I lived a life of supernatural abundance, longevity, and unprecedented increase. Brother Warren, like me, God picked you for the toughest challenges because he trusts you to stand. The rain falls on the just and unjust alike. Now, go in peace and have faith.*

God sees you, and he understands. You shall receive your measure of beauty for ashes. It shall come to pass, be it unto to you.

Love,

Job

Public Grandeur, Private Pain

For most of my life, I was unsettled with my sexuality. I very vividly remember—as far back as two years old—looking at other boys and noticing an attraction. Though I found boys attractive, I didn't marvel in my feelings. As a matter of fact, I hated my feelings because I just wanted to be normal, or what I perceived normal to be. I wished God had let that cup, that assignment, pass from me □. I had a thorn in my flesh, and I wanted no part of it! I prayed, and God, by creating in my spirit, gave me the response, "not yet." Then I realized, to truly be free, I had to rid myself of the shame. I decided to expose myself and thus regain power over my haunting secrets—and boy, did I have secrets. In short order, my life changed. The one thing we can all count on and should anticipate is change...there's a time for everything. Either you anticipate and adapt to change, or you shall become irrelevant. According to the scripture, "To everything there is a season, and a time to every purpose under the heaven:

A time to be born, and a time to die; a time to plant, and a time to pluck up that which is planted; a time to kill, and a time to heal; a time to break down, and a time to build up; a time to weep, and a time to laugh; a time to mourn, and a time to dance; a time to cast away stones, and a time to gather stones together; a time to embrace, and a time to refrain from embracing; a time to get, and a time to lose; a time to keep, and a time to cast away; a time to rend, and a time to sew; a time to keep silence, and a time to speak; a time to love, and a time to hate; a time of war, and a time of peace. (Ecclesiastes 3:2-8 [KJV])

I feared judgment and unconsciously sought validation from folks who didn't have a hell or heaven to house me. I pretended; I shielded my secrets with masks of many colors, styles, and shapes. My origin story dictated that I should marry a woman, have kids, buy a dog and a house with a picket fence, and live happily ever after. That narrative was reinforced by my military career. As a matter of fact, I served during the entire period of "Don't ask, don't tell."

I experienced the good, bad, and ugly. The hurt, pain, disappointment, rejection, dejection, anger, and frustration all had me bound. I was cracked, but not broken. It was all part of the process.

I tried so hard. I tried so hard to believe in what I prayed, what I proclaimed. I learned my prayers weren't enough...my due diligence wasn't enough...my preparations weren't enough...my declarations and proclamations just didn't seem to be enough!

As my faith faded, I believed people—influencers—were the equalizers. People of significant and noteworthy lineage called the shots! Like Job, I wondered "Where is God?" I had to let my faith roar so loudly I couldn't hear what doubt was saying. I was determined not to allow my lying eyes to fool me. After campaigning unsuccessfully for nearly three years, I had nothing else to give, even to myself. I was broke and had a mountain of debt. My faith was drastically shaken. I felt like giving up. But God spoke to me through the songwriter Smokie Norful: "I see you, and yes, I understand." Every time I got in the car, that song seemed to play on the radio. Those words ministered to my mind and soul and helped me hold on to my faith in God.

I also kept a quote from Lao Tze in my mind: "Watch your thoughts; they become words. Watch your words; they become actions. Watch your actions; they become habits. Watch your habits; they become character. Watch your character; it becomes your destiny."

I moved to Atlanta to live with friends. I felt homeless. I had no place to call my own, but I held on to the little hope I did have. I was low, low, low! Nevertheless, I leaned on the words, "Though you slay me, yet will I worship..." No matter my trials, never before had I been hungry, without a nice place to lay my head, without healthcare, or gone without my essential needs met. Certainly, that was not the case now. I just believed I was to do more, have more, more influence, lead more. I knew God had more for me than just enough.

I also knew I was on the potter's wheel, pregnant with possibilities, but, once again, there were no manifestations of movement. I cried, I chose depression and isolation, and my heart ached. I was humbled. I realized I'd been entitled. The onlookers only saw my iceberg of success...they saw a tall, fit, well-put-together, handsome Black man projecting outward confidence. They saw the surface. What they did not see was what laid beneath...pain, disappointment, failure, many unsuccessful attempts at success. They didn't see my struggles, my rejections, the no's, the heartbreak, and fears. Folks often look at your "glorious" circumstances and desire what you have. Those same people refuse to understand the costs—what it takes for you to be in the space you are in. They want your green, plushy grass but do not want the water bill that comes with having a nicely manicured lawn.

I asked myself, "Why shouldn't I have to overcome?" My healing was in my vulnerabilities. I had to acknowledge my pain, then submit to the healer. For me, that healer was almighty God, my redeemer. The tricks the enemy sent to destroy me, God used to set me up—He set me up for peace, joy, mercy, and grace. Those intangible things had more meaning than anything else. Although I felt like God had forgotten about me, I realized God allows everything for our spiritual growth, and me and God alone are a majority. God reminded me, "I am the God who hung the stars, turned night into day. I healed the crippled and made the blind to see. I stopped time for Joshua and accelerated water into wine, so don't test my gangsta."

I was in the right place, it was the right time, but I had the wrong mindset. I had to cut the umbilical cord to depression, bitterness, sorrow, and harboring hurt and unforgiveness ☐.

I made a choice for my healing. Outstretched before God, I was a child of possibilities, not one at risk. After I was told I should have been a derelict during my first mental health therapy treatment, I changed my mindset. I decided it's not what others say about me that's important; it's what *I* say about me that prevails! All the Spirit required of me was obedience and trust in Him. When I did those things, in an instant, I was blessed beyond measure. I was told "no" so many times, but I'd finally reached my "yes," and my measure was pressed down, shaken together, and running over.

I didn't understand. My circumstances didn't make sense. I was thirsty for understanding; I desperately craved it. That's when I was forced to lean on faith. I then considered the letters from The Virgin Mary, Job, and King David. I began to understand that God picked me because he knew he could trust me. In my spirit, I heard the words, "Trust in the Lord with all thine heart; and lean not unto thine own understanding. In all thy ways acknowledge *Him* and *He* shall direct your path" (Proverbs 3:5-6 [KJV]). I then reminded myself to be patient, be at peace, and let God bless you in His time...nothing will stop God's plans for your life, your destiny.

When He picked me, I didn't get many details...actually, I don't think I got any, LOL □. God spoke to my heart, saying, "Be still, be quiet, know I am God, and keep the faith."

Chapter Summary

❖ Speak life over yourself—words are important.

❖ The truth shall set you free.

❖ Don't ask, and I won't tell.

❖ My healing rested in my vulnerability.

❖ The energy you put out is the energy that will be returned to you. The seeds you plant shall be the harvest you reap.

❖ It's not what others say about me that's important, it's what *I* say about me that prevails.

❖ A spiritual power exists in my universe. I can't do justice in explaining my faith in God; my faith is everything to me. No matter what comes, I'm in it to win it!

❖ Life is a maze—and no one gets out alive.

❖ Let go and let God in—forgive yourself and stop looking in the rearview mirror.

❖ It's all part of the process. Being on the potter's wheel seems unbearable—be steadfast and unmovable. Your time, your due season, your "suddenly" is nigh.

A Letter from My Older Self

Hey fella,

I've been meaning to text you for some time now. I am so thankful you're holding on to your faith in God—your spirituality. Thanks for your obedience. And thank God for His mercy and grace. You've had quite a journey so far.

You've proven that where a person starts doesn't dictate where they'll finish. Time and time again, you were given lemons and found a way to turn them into lemonade. No matter the trial or tribulation, you stood strong—like a tree planted by the water, you would not be moved. I know you're thankful to our younger self for the strength and courage he passed on to you.

I want you to know I'm grateful to you because you'll pass an even higher level of consciousness on to me □□.

Early on, you recognized and believed your inner captain is an eagle. Thanks for setting the conditions for our impact on the world. I have seen your tears and your courage to be emotionally available. You have been blessed in so many ways. We have our beautiful daughters, their mom, and our authentic friends. We've had a great career in the Army and a run for the U.S. Congress. We have been blessed educationally, financially, spiritually, and mentally. You are healthy and wealthy in so many ways! You're an author; you'll continue to impact the multitude of God's people and positively change the lives of people all over the world. Not to mention our Madea—wow, she was no joke and very necessary, setting the conditions for our joyous victory dance.

God continues to prepare you for unprecedented success—He favors you. In the waiting period, you must keep the faith. You mustn't allow your lying eyes to trick you. God picked you because He knows you will stand and because He trusts you—your time is coming once again. You will be thrust into a life you and others will marvel over, knowing the hand of God has prospered you mightily. So, don't forget: thoughts become things. Satan □ wants to attack your mindset, so be aware. You must slay yourself daily, arise with a fresh anointing, and adorn yourself with the whole armor of God.

Continue treating people with dignity and respect. You have the gift of connecting authentically with people; strangers quickly recognize your spiritual gifts. Your positive energy is infectious, and you are wise beyond your years. You diligently hunt the good stuff—keep hunting, keep seeking, and you shall keep flourishing.

You got on the threshing floor, where the chaff was separated from the wheat and the chaff was burned. You did your work. You did what needed to be done to attain a higher level of consciousness. You acknowledged your pain and your weaknesses and did more work. It was through your vulnerabilities I was made whole.

My healing rested in your weaknesses. The typical nature of people is often sinister. Their default is to be critical, find fault in others, and often be hypocritical, always looking to remove the speck from your eye □

rather than dealing with the plank in their own. It's not what others say about us that's important. It's what you say about us that prevails. You've learned to not carry on with things and people who don't contribute to us reaching our destiny. It's easy to be baited by negative forces. That's not to say adversity wasn't a part of our plight—much to the contrary! I fervently believe all things work together for good; rain falls on the just and unjust. It is well. You're divorced and not bitter. You lost an election; all is well. You lost loved ones; all is well. People walked out of your life, praise God; all is well. You've been treated unkindly and unfairly, been talked about and made fun of; nevertheless, all is well. You were rejected, denied, didn't get the job you wanted, haven't seen all your dreams realized—no problem. I'm at peace, not worried; all shall be well. So, until it's my time to lead us to our final destination, stay the course, run your race with the kind of vigor and enthusiasm only you can, and know I'm always rooting for you!

Love,

Your Older Self □□□□□

I Am Enough

I am blessed, talented, amazing, forgiven, kind, strong, favored, healed, ordained for greatness, gifted, more than a conqueror, God's masterpiece, prosperous, wise, healthy, creative, confident. I am all God says I am. In the words of Marianne Williamson, "Our greatest fear is not that we are inadequate. Our deepest fear is that we are powerful beyond measure. It is our light, not our darkness, that most frightens us."

I made up my mind I will speak life over my circumstances. I gave up on seeking validation from people who had no power over my blessings.

Because of my early childhood trauma and experiences, I built defenses that didn't serve me well. I accepted behavior contrary to decency and

147

honor. My own behavior was sabotaging my future. I was angry □, envious, calculating, and emotionally empty. I was being tripped by chihuahuas and easily distracted by foolery and nonsense. I concerned myself with far too many things that didn't matter. A dear mentor said to me once, "If it's not going to matter in a hundred years, to hell with it." To occupy my time and dismiss my own issues, I took on the energy and issues of most anyone I encountered with the goal of "fixing" them. Those assignments didn't come from God. I was overwhelmed, operating according to my own agenda. I didn't know I was empathic, in a metaphysical sense—I feel and am significantly affected by the energies and emotions of others—until years later. In reflection, I recall being drained most of the time because unconsciously, I allowed others to transfer whatever they had going on to me. I learned to say to beleaguered people, "Do not bring your burdens here and leave them; I am not the Lord" LOL □.

I tried to be all things to all I encountered because I so desperately wanted a family—people to love and care about me. A traditional family is the one thing I feel like I missed out on in life. Aside from my daughters, what I wanted more than professional success was a family to call my own. Of the many successes I experienced and continue to experience in my purpose-driven life, family still seems to escape me □. God reminds me, His grace is sufficient.

Notwithstanding, I never really had someone to say, "I love you" or to hug me in the spirit of agape love. In America, particularly in the Black community, it's a sign of weakness if you tell a boy you love them, or give them a hug, or validate their emotions. I truly needed and wanted innocent hugs, love, and emotionally cultivating care. I grew up with depression, though hidden and subdued. I never dealt with the fact that I was abandoned by my mother. I suppressed all that hurt and pain. When I got married, I still hadn't dealt with that pain. I was still hurting, though not outwardly. Inside, I was a mess! I wasn't able to be vulnerable with my ex-wife. On an emotional and communicative level, I wasn't able to meet my ex-wife's needs, and she wasn't able to meet mine.

I was always cautious about sharing because folks are quick to judge others while their own lives are jacked up. I believe many people would have suggested to me, "Just be open and transparent." But being vulnerable, sharing my fears and innermost pains during that season, was not an option. That level of transparency is tough and requires a lot of prework. It's not an easy feat by any means. I carried a lot of baggage, which caused me to have a lack of trust when it came to being vulnerable. My origin story—the reasons for the costumes I wore—dominated. I was filled with shame and guilt I tried in so many ways to hide. I became the greatest makeup artist of all-time. I used my titles, my status, and my degrees to disguise my pain...to distract and deceive. But God spoke to my spirit and told me, "I won't deal with your representative. Give me all of you, or nothing at all."

Speaking of representatives, I've had a few, LOL ☐ ☐. I am not proud of all my choices. As a matter of fact, I've made many poor choices. Nevertheless, I am triumphant because of my tests, which allow me to share my powerful testimony! I can see very clearly where God used every experience for my growth and good. God favored me in spite of my enemies—the naysayers tried, but God wouldn't let them triumph over me □□□□□□□□□□□. I made a choice not to let people rent space in my head for free.

The thorn in my flesh left me ashamed and questioning my sexuality. I was held hostage by the negative narratives of "you can't," "you won't," "you haven't," and "you don't."

I am reminded of a powerful quote by John Newton: "I'm not what I ought to be, nor what I want to be. I am not what I hope to be, but still I am not what I used to be. But by the grace and mercy of God, I am that I am."

I never confronted or reconciled with the violation of my young body back in fifth grade. I harbored that experience and thought it was best forgotten. I adopted the old adage, "Let sleeping dogs lie." As a matter of fact, I wouldn't speak of that experience again for nearly forty years.

It caused me to completely lack confidence in my sexuality. I just wanted to be happy while making every effort to meet the expectations of my "community," which included the church, hypocritical family members, and friends. I also wanted to remain safe from the negative associations of being a man who was attracted to both men and woman. I wouldn't dare reveal my secret, fearing harsh verbal rebukes like, "Girl, I knew this was too good to be true. This peanut butter packin', pillow-biting gay motha'fucka got me fucked up if he thinks…" This call and text would go out to her girlfriends everywhere.

The anticipated pain from soul-piercing denouncements were more than I was willing to bear. I just didn't have the courage to jettison my masks. I treated myself poorly by not valuing who God said I was. I didn't value who God created me to be. Hell, I didn't *know* who God created me to be. I didn't know the eagle in me, ordained by God. I suited up with the whole armor of God and believed no matter what negative things others said about me, they had no power to stop God's blessings in my life. I knew I couldn't control the actions of others, but I could make every effort to control my response. What folks didn't know was God was doing a new thing in me, and I couldn't allow myself to be tricked by the proverbial enemy—I had to maintain my peace.

I continue on my journey to a higher level of enlightenment and courage, incrementally. I wish for myself the courage to know love—intimately and without borders.

Chapter Summary

❖ We are powerful beyond measure.

❖ Don't get tripped by the Chihuahuas—keep your head up and avoid sweating the small stuff.

❖ Naysayers are envious. Treat their opposition like food—take what your mind needs for nourishment and crap the rest out.Water seeks its level—rise to yours by associating with good measure.

❖ Luck is when preparedness meets opportunity. Show up and show out.

❖ Try to smile—even when you're hurting.

Lost & Found

I found my dad in 1996, shortly after I became a dad myself, with the help of *The Ricki Lake Show*. I had written to her to ask if she and her team could help me find my dad. My Madea, as well as everyone else who knew anything about the man, had since passed away, so all I had to go on was his name.

My momma kept me from knowing my dad. She told me he was killed in the Vietnam War. For so many years, as I roamed around the world, I saw men I thought could have been my dad. Like the ugly duckling, I wanted so badly to ask them, "Are you my dad?" I knew in my heart, regardless of what I'd been told, my dad was out there somewhere, and one day, I was gonna find him!

To my amazement, my dad and I were reunited. That unification was amazing. When I saw him, we embraced and cried tears of joy. Our meeting was exhilarating. We embraced some more. He stood about six foot, four inches tall and weighed around 185 pounds—a slim, fit, dark-skinned, handsome man. When I finally got to see him, I knew instantly his genes were dominant. As I looked at him, it felt like I was looking in a mirror—my other twin (many say Ashley, my youngest daughter, is my twin).

Since that first meeting, we've had a lot of good times together. My dad and I have enjoyed the time spent building our still fresh relationship, and I've loved every moment of it. I've met so many new family members including aunts, siblings, and a host of cousins. I learned about his early childhood and how he was mistreated terribly by his dad. Our stories were quite similar. I'm so very glad God granted us the mindset to break the family cycles of dysfunction and pain.

My dad chose to delete negativity from his mind. He enlisted in the U.S. Army as an engineer, served in Vietnam twice, and enjoyed an exceptionally fast-tracked and distinguished career. During his marriage, my dad had two daughters and two sons; I enjoy a great relationship with my sisters—my dad's two daughters. I've never met his other two sons. Having met my dad inspired me even more to be the best dad I could be. I also wanted to be the best family man I could be, but I didn't achieve that victory.

Although I have my two daughters, and I'm now divorced, I still long for family. I look around at Thanksgiving and Christmas, and I watch other families. While I have been amazingly blessed in so many areas of my life, family is the one thing that escaped me, perhaps as a result of being so broken at a time in life when others were building their own. Nevertheless, God made up for that in many ways, and I am pleased. I have an extended family consisting of people who are not necessarily related to me by blood. When I celebrate, I celebrate with my nontraditional family. In my heart and mind, they are my family; they provide nurturing, love, and the embraces and validation I longed for during the many years of void and feeling empty. They are jewels that add intangible value, unmatched and absolutely priceless. Many of my relationships were born and forged during my career in the military, my Congressional campaign, mentoring, teaching, and of course, parenting my daughters.

For many years after my divorce, and probably during my marriage, I was afraid of intimate relationships. At that time in life, I created distractions; I operated a small business and did very well, but I was barely holding it together emotionally.

I used the care of my daughters and the demands of my business as a crutch because I was afraid to be vulnerable and to bare my heart and soul to another person. I feared being rejected again—the first rejection was by my own momma □. I also feared not being accepted. I very much would like to be married again. My ideal spouse would be someone who, first and foremost, is a compassionate communicator. Someone who loves God, who loves people, and who has a great sense of humility. My ideal mate is bold, courageous, and empathetic; someone who is unafraid and unapologetic. A person who would accept me and my daughters without equivocation. A person of depth—sex will not sustain me, and I suspect the same goes for most sane people. I must have intellectual, mental, and intimate stimulation in order for anyone to keep my attention.

I want someone who shares in my passion, who has dreams I could be a part of, and someone who would allow me to be a "leader mate" in their life. What I mean by the term "leader mate" is someone who recognizes that we are both leaders in our family. No one person would try to dominate or rule over the other. We would be helpmates to one another. I absolutely believe in love and monogamy—I believe in chivalry, LOL □. I believe in love so strongly because my grandmother taught me God is love. Without knowing or having a relationship with God, I don't believe one can really have a loving relationship with anyone else. You have to understand the source of love. Once that happens, you are able to begin the process of loving yourself, and perhaps even falling in love with someone else. One thing I learned along my life's journey is that unless you are willing to be vulnerable and self-aware, it's hard to fall in love. Although love shouldn't be scary, for me, it is. The level of vulnerability required is quite scary. I offer an analogy as a perspective.

Every day, one goes to the bank and makes a deposit. Over a period of time, a nice nest egg is built. However, one day, you go to the bank to make an emotional withdrawal because you're depleted and learn there's nothing to withdraw. All the investing you did, all the deposits you made were for naught, and now, you must start over. You are emotionally bankrupt. Those kinds of ideas, that mindset, prevents me from availing my whole self.

Like me, many men, for whatever reason, form defenses, and we take those defenses into our adulthood. For me, those defenses caused me to build emotional barriers and to hide my vulnerabilities. While I really want to fall in love again and have a family, I am extremely cautious and nervous. I decided before I could love anyone else, I needed to fall in love with myself. A few years back, I did my work—I fell in love with *me*!

The older I get, the more I become my true self. I'm not very tolerant of what I call "extra"—all the drama and games broken-spirited people play. I believe when you have a mate, a partner and a friend all in one, who is able to be vulnerable and talk with you about anything and everything, without judgment, then it provides for a level of unwavering monogamy, vulnerability, truth, and transparency. However, when "relationships" become "official," whether consummated by marriage or when seriously dating, men and women begin to treat each other with less dignity and respect and adopt a sense of complacency. In my experience, women want to be respected and empowered, but they feel it necessary to disrespect and emasculate their man, trying hard to reform him into what they want him to be. It would be grand if prayers went up asking God, "Reveal to me what I'm to be to him and what he's to be to me, and how." When true love exists, according to the scriptures:

Love is patient, love is kind. It does not envy, it does not boast, it is not proud. It does not dishonor others, it is not self-seeking, it is not easily angered, it keeps no record of wrongs. Love does not delight in evil but rejoices with the truth. It always protects, always trusts, always hopes, always perseveres. (1 Corinthians 13:4-7 [NIV])

What the scripture didn't note is that love is hard, and it shall be tested.

Men, on the other hand, often seek to leverage the scripture, "Wives, submit yourselves unto your own husbands, as unto the lord" (Ephesians 5:22 [KJV]). What they miss is that the scripture goes on to read, "Men, love your wives as Jesus loves the church." Moreover, you need to understand scripture in its ancient meaning. This ancient letter to a church in Ephesus wasn't written in modern English, and much of what we assume when we translate "submit," is definitely misleading. In this context, the ancient word, "hupotassomai," or submit, most closely means "Wives, support your husbands," "Wives, deploy yourselves in support of your husbands," or "Wives, arrange yourselves for battle for your husbands."

Many are not self-aware enough, not vulnerable enough, and haven't done the work to rid themselves of their demons. Most don't really love themselves and can in no way love someone else. Many people are spiritually broken and emotionally unavailable. We seek characteristics in people we don't possess ourselves. We spend so much time talking and very little time listening, always trying to prove our point and be our own version of right, SMDH ☐☐♂☐. While words are important, deeds are where the power is.

Both parties in a relationship cannot always be in charge and always be right. The wiser one must take a collaborative, perhaps submissive, role and ditch what others think should be done. Seek God; ask God to order your steps and guide your spirit. Consider this—we look and strive so diligently to have a meaningful and fulfilling relationship, and we say we desire an equally yoked mate. However, we skip the "relations" phase—truly getting to know the person, understanding their mental, spiritual, psychological, emotional, and financial circumstances. We just jump right into the "ship" part with no life vest on. We fall overboard, we can't swim, and we drown. All because we started sleeping with the enemy and wondered afterward, after being in too deep, who in the hell this person is.

Then, disrespect, intolerance, and impatience take over. Men start referring to their woman as "bitch," and women start calling their man "motherfucka" and "his sorry, no-good ass." We become so tempestuous and mean-spirited. Hurt people hurt people. Is that any way to build and sustain a meaningful and long-term relationship? Even in a joking manner, name-calling is unhealthy and will set a course for assured destruction. We play so many games, bring so much drama, and keep so many secrets from the ones we profess to love. Instead of being transparent and talking to our mate, we often choose to holla at our "boy" or chop it up with our "homegirl" about issues and challenges. We move ourselves into a passive-aggressive state and move away from confronting our mate. I promise you; you can talk to your friends all you want, but no one else can reconcile the issue except you and the person concerned. We complain about not being happy. Couples are not responsible for making each other happy—happiness lives within. It is an individual responsibility. I wasn't happy, and I blamed others; I was deficient and found every reason to escape my responsibility. While doing my work, I truly became emotionally intelligent, a gift you can only receive from God! I started being grateful for everything and every experience.

We take so much for granted. When we lose an amazingly wonderful spirit God provided for us, we regret, cry, and feel sad and lonely, wishing we could reset and start over. But by then it's too late! Very rarely do we truly appreciate the value our mates add, no matter how small or how big. This kind of fuckery is done in the name of being right, in the name of unnecessary drama, stubbornness, lack of humility and self-awareness, and shit yo' homegirl or homeboy said—misery loves company. The enemy comes to kill, steal, and destroy! *Stop!* If someone wants out of your life, let them go—they were not ordained to be a part of your destiny. Rise above the games, nonsense, and drama. Elevate yourselves to the realm of excellence designed especially for you.

"People will come and go in life, but the person in the mirror will be there forever. Be good to yourself!" (author unknown).

Being married is a blessing, and I believe the sanctity of marriage is under serious attack. We are puzzled by why our younger generations are straying away from marriage, choosing to forego marriage and "shack up," as my Madea would say. That's because they've seen what us older generations have done to the sanctity of marriage. We've made it so marriage looks like a dead end, a prison, a sentence of unhappiness and dishonesty. They want no part of our examples of marriage, nor do they realize being argumentative, disagreeable, defensive, and withdrawn won't resolve anything in *any* relationship—married or not.

I'm often reminded of the calls from men and women who were on planes on 9/11 leaving voicemails for loved ones for the last time. We don't know the state of the relationships prior to those folks boarding those planes. What we do know is they'll never have another opportunity to say, "I'm sorry," or "Please forgive me." Please don't take people for granted; to live with the pain of unnecessary sorrow is not worth your peace. Tomorrow is truly not guaranteed; we're all on loan from God. So, live every day to the fullest. Most of us will only get one chance to die.

In my marriage, I failed to prioritize what was really important because I didn't know how. I wish I'd been familiar with *The Rocks, Pebbles, and Sand* story, as recounted below by StorlieTelling.com.

"A philosophy professor stood before his class and had some items in front of him. When class began, wordlessly he picked up a large empty mayonnaise jar and proceeded to fill it with rocks right to the top, rocks about two inches in diameter. He then asked the students if the jar was full? They agreed that it was. So, the professor then picked up a box of pebbles and poured them into the jar. He shook the jar lightly. The pebbles, of course, rolled into the open areas between the rocks. The students laughed. He asked his students again if the jar was full? They agreed that yes, it was. The professor then picked up a box of sand and poured it into the jar. Of course, the sand filled up everything else. He then asked once more if the jar was full. The students responded with a unanimous yes. 'Now,' said the professor, 'I want you to recognize that this is your life.

"The rocks are the important things—your family, your partner, your health, your children—anything that is so important to you, that if it were lost, you would be nearly destroyed. The pebbles are the other things in life that matter, but on a smaller scale. The pebbles represent things like your job, your house, your car. The sand is everything else. The small stuff.

"If you put the sand or the pebbles into the jar first, there is no room for the rocks. The same goes for your life. If you spend all your energy and time on the small stuff—material things—you will never have room for the things that are truly most important. Pay attention to the things that are critical in your life. Play with your children. Take your partner out dancing. There will always be time to go to work, clean the house, give a dinner party, or fix the disposal. Take care of the rocks first—the things that really matter. Set your priorities. The rest is just pebbles and sand.'"

This story would have certainly aided me in making better choices to preserve my core family. Perhaps we'd have been the family I dreamed of, or perhaps we wouldn't have, as our challenges ran deep. What was exhilarating was learning about her pregnancy.

When Lisa told me she was pregnant, I cried and instantly became extraordinarily overprotective of her. After all, she was carrying my child, my most prized blessing from God. We weren't married at the time. However, where I come from, my upbringing dictated I must propose and marry her—I did. In the first trimester of *our* pregnancy, Lisa called me while at 1-2-1 General Hospital in Seoul, South Korea, crying. She told me the doctor told her to go home, lie down, and come to grips with his opinion that she was going to have a miscarriage. Since Lisa was hemorrhaging, the doctor concluded she would not carry our baby to term and the pregnancy would self-terminate.

Lisa and I were both stationed in the Second Infantry Division, at Camp Casey, near the DMZ. We had to remain discrete because I was a lieutenant, a commissioned officer, and Lisa was a sergeant, a noncommissioned officer. Moreover, I was the aide-de-camp to the assistant division commander, one of my most favorite generals. When I heard her crying immediately after her appointment, my heart sank. I unequivocally and immediately rejected the doctor's opinion! In the days to follow, Lisa and I returned to the hospital for a visit. I told the doctor I rejected his opinion and demanded he do everything he could to ensure our baby was going to survive—he did. That spring, Lisa and I, along with our unborn baby, did a permanent change of duty station to Fort Sill, Oklahoma.

During the weeks and months prior to our baby's birth, I experienced so many symptoms of a sympathetic pregnancy—vomiting, fatigue, nausea, and unusual cravings. That fall, Lisa gave birth to our beautiful daughter. Ashley was born at Reynolds Army Hospital. During labor and delivery, as I held Lisa's hand and comforted her, I had the worse back pain... hell, *I* needed an epidural, LMAO ☐☐☐. I know many have not been blessed with that kind of beauty from God and may never have such an experience with their own child.

Before Ashley was born, I decided I was going to be the best father I could be to her. I committed to leveraging my experiences of love and pain to establish a foundation of Godly love for my daughter. I was unequivocal in my determination to protect her, nurture her, and love her with everything—with every fiber of my being.

I met Brittany, Lisa's daughter from a previous relationship, after Lisa and I got married, and while we were still expecting Ashley. When we moved to Oklahoma with our newborn in tow, Brittany came with us. It was the first time we all lived together under one roof.

I remember it so clearly; the memories bring joy to my heart.

Lisa and I were both in the Army and stationed in Oklahoma. One day, after moving into our newly renovated military quarters, Brittany asked me, "Will I be able to call you Daddy?" At the time,

Brittany was in second grade. I told her I would not expect her to call me anything else but daddy. I was immensely humbled and grateful God allowed me to be the dad of two amazingly beautiful and warm-spirited daughters!

Lisa and I were legally separated when Brittany started high school in tenth grade.

Unfortunately, and shortly after, Lisa and I divorced, but I was so blessed to continue being a dad to my two daughters. I continued to raise both my daughters after the separation. One of my life's greatest blessings was, is, and will always be the opportunity to be a dad. I was very stern and, undoubtedly, a strict disciplinarian. I don't think my daughters liked me when they were growing up because I provided a lot of structure in our household. They clearly understood I was the parent, and they were the children. I did not do a lot of negotiating. I was preparing them for the day I might not be around. Preparing them to be strong and courageous, God-fearing, respectable young ladies. I knew I couldn't teach them how to be women, but I could teach them conduct and behavior.

They were latchkey kids; they came home from school, got a snack, and started their homework, and by that time, I would come home. Then we would eat together at the dinner table. They always tried to convince me to put a television in the kitchen. However, I was not a fan; I believed dinner was our family time. They'd tell me about their day and let me know how they needed my help. After dinner, I would help them with their homework. Up through tenth grade, they both had bedtimes. They had to go to bed by nine p.m. because I understood that if they went to bed too late, they would not be alert, present, and focused in class the next day. My two daughters are amazing. They are focused and driven, and they've been extremely supportive. They make me proud to be their dad.

I made every effort to teach my daughters and remind myself to be kind, work hard, stay humble, smile often, be loyal, be honest, travel when possible, never stop learning, be thankful, and love always.

I made sure to tell my daughters daily that I loved them. I spoke life and victory over their lives, reminding them often whose they were and how amazing they were. I taught them who they were before the world had a chance to teach them who they were not!

Warren's daughters: Brittany and Ashley.

I told them they were beautiful, and their hair and skin were beautiful. I hugged them often. We prayed together often. We attended church together often. I also gave them some latitude and longitude to explore their strengths. I wasn't so hard when it came to Brittany telling me she really wasn't interested in college, and she wanted to be a beautician. In the same spirit, speaking her truth,

Ashley told me she wanted to play sports, even though I wanted her to take ballet and gymnastics. Brittany attended college and became a beautician, and Ashley played soccer and ran track. I really tried to expose them to a variety of activities. They are amazingly smart and talented young Black ladies. I believe I encouraged and reinforced their confidence.

Another thing I tried to avoid was exposing them to my casual dating situations. I rarely brought people around, with the exception of those who were role models and who had no ulterior motives. The greatest thing I did differently from my upbringing was to tell my daughters frequently how beautiful, smart, and talented they were. I also told them how proud I was of them focusing on school, being respectful to teachers, and being kind to their peers.

My biggest fear as a parent was someone compromising my daughters in a way that steals their innocence or disrespects them as Black women. Earlier in this book, I shared the pain that was associated with my childhood growing up in Alabama. One of the reasons I had so much hurt and pain is because I felt like I wasn't protected. Some of my own family members bullied me about having darker skin than the rest of my family; I didn't pass the brown paper-bag test. I wasn't protected by my mother when she abandoned me.

Although the abandonment was like no other pain I've felt, it was a blessing in disguise. God knew exactly what He was doing, He was preparing me for greatness □□□□□. Even though I hurt, I smiled. God was preparing me for fatherhood; to be a good dad to my daughters—one who could and would always protect them. I love being a dad, and when my babies were growing up, I always kept them close. I made no space to trust anyone. I wasn't protected when it came to my innocence, and I'd be damned if I was going to take any chances with someone violating my babies!

To this day, I still give my daughters relationship advice. Their mates may be similar to me—after all, I've heard a girl often marries a man similar in character to their dad. Over the years, I would always ask my daughters not to let any man compromise them—not to tolerate or ignore any disrespect or physical abuse. If their future mates can't be team players and help to support and endorse their careers, then they should ask themselves if that's a situation they really want. I want their mates to be respectful and respectable. I want their mates to be rooted in faith and spirituality. I want their mates to be compassionate and sensitive. I want them to have come from a family where they experienced a lot of love. People carry their baggage around with them. So, I would personally desire each of their mates to be mentally secure, emotionally available, to be strong, professional, and honorable Black men. My truth is my truth. Notwithstanding, whatever the race of their mate, it's obviously their choice to make. I'll always love them unconditionally regardless of who they love.

I have big hopes and dreams for my daughters. I wish them peace, God's most precious blessings, love, honor, kindness, laughter, gratitude, joy, empathy, and the ability to forgive. My enduring advice to them is to treat folks as they ought to be treated—with dignity and respect. Take God everywhere you go. Work hard and be about your business as a woman. Marry well and serve your community with poise and grace, and don't cast your pearl before swine.

Being a single dad was a life-changing experience. I gained a better understanding of the struggles of Black women in the world. When Lisa and I legally separated, I insisted, and thankfully Lisa agreed, that I keep our daughters—I felt I had the best chance to ensure proper exposure and future success for them. I needed my daughters with me. I couldn't breathe without them. When I became a single dad, I quickly began to appreciate more deeply my daughters' mom and other mothers. Black men receive lots of pats on the back and praise for being single dads because it's not the norm. Black women, who have been single parents for hundreds of years, never receive pats on the back. Actually, to the contrary, Black single moms are quickly criticized, while deadbeat dads go unscathed and are excused without any accountability.

Black single moms rarely get accolades of appreciation or are told thank you because it's expected of them to make the sacrifice. That was a life-changing realization that caused me to have a renewed and profound respect and advocacy for women at large, but particularly Black women. Today, Lisa and I remain friends.

Chapter Summary

❖ Do not take your loved ones for granted—you'll live to regret it. Tomorrow is not guaranteed; we're all on loan from God.

❖ Love is challenging—though it shouldn't, it truly does hurt and shall be tested.

❖ Be unapologetically vulnerable—stop the games. Focus on the "relations." Prepare to board the "ship" after you have the skills to stay afloat if the ship goes down.

❖ Ensure your "rocks" are properly nurtured—make the main thing the main thing.

❖ Be what you desire—respectful, peaceful, joyful, honorable, kind, loving, and mature.

❖ Do not be too prideful to apologize.

❖ Allow your eaglets to spread their wings and fly; set the conditions for their success.

❖ Teach yourself and your children who they are before the streets and the world teach you and them who you and they are not.

❖ Nurturing and love are intangible jewels—they are priceless.

❖ God is the source of love—learn to love yourself so you can love others.

❖ Honor women—especially mothers. They do a lot!

❖ Parent-child relationships can be redefined when children reach maturity. Kids want and need wise parents; trying to be their friend too soon will yield poor dividends.

The Rest of the Story

I'm my lived experiences, and I suspect in the lives of others, temptation creeps in, provoking options to choose the easy wrong over the hard right. Some may even challenge what right is and from who's perspective. Or what truth is and from who's perspective. Truth can be scary and even uncomfortable. Nevertheless, I continue in *my* truths. I've elected to leave those deeper questions for a dissertation perhaps. But in the here and now, I present the rest of my story.

Growing up in Alabama, on Wildman Bottom Road was fun when my Madea's family would come for Sunday dinner and like an abyss when no one was around. After everyone left, started their own families and careers, it was me, Madea, and Uncle

Bud. My Madea's brothers also lived off that winding dirt road and one of her brothers had a grandson he was raising.

Occasionally, he would come over to Madea's house—we were playmates. That playtime was so emotionally satisfying, as the only things I did were work on the farm, go to church, and go to school. The times, though not often, Steve and I spent together playing, hunting, running through pastures, fishing, and laughing were so memorable and awesome! He was my one and only best friend.

My Uncle Bud, who was a schoolteacher, spent a lot of time with his male students, and not much time with me. As I recall, he was also a basketball coach. He occasionally included me in extracurricular activities like movies, basketball games, and football games. He invited one boy to live with us at my Madea's house. Anyone outside looking in would have easily thought I was the outsider, the black sheep. That boy, and other boys, got most all of Uncle Bud's attention, time, and resources. Though I was his nephew by blood, for some reason, I wasn't worthy of him investing in me.

It was one more thing reinforcing the trauma concerning my abandonment and molestation.

When you are in a quiet place and you're the only one around day in and day out, it's difficult. On the farm in Alabama, I used to pray daily because I felt so alone. There was too much pain associated with Alabama. I felt like God delivered me from evil when I finally left the region □□. I would pray to God, "Lord, I want to be a soldier. I want to be a dad." I remember praying to be the President of the United States of America. I also prayed for God to take me far, far away from that place in Alabama—and he did indeed! At that time, I didn't even understand how many states there were. I had no clue about what being the President of the United States was all about, but I was just so fascinated with politics even then. At that point, of course, I didn't realize my life would be entangled with politics and my love of service would be so poignant.

I've been blessed with being a father and a career soldier, and I'm excited about what God continues to do in my life. I think there is a horrible connotation associated with the word "politics" or "politician." I'm not interested in becoming a politician. I want to continue to be a servant leader and eventually become an elected official.

My grandmama, with the rearing she gave me and the work ethic she instilled in me, impacted my life significantly. However, the greatest life-changing experience I had—one that drives my passion to this day—was serving our country, whether it was as an Army officer, as the chief of staff at the department of interior making every effort to be a good steward of federal taxpayer dollars or working in the United States Senate for a number of very prominent senators. Those experiences reinforced and validated that where I came from didn't dictate where I could go—my mindset did. It's about the work. It's about having been able to serve my country in the garments of American warriors and being *proud* to serve my country. Those kinds of experiences reinforced my can-do mindset. Whatever else I choose to do, I shall do it well because I have solid examples of proving my worth and my contributions to the world. No matter what consternation I faced, I pressed on.

The military is a great place to serve; it changed my life forever! Many people in America believe our uniformed services are trustworthy, fair, and equitable. I don't believe most senior uniformed military leaders take that level of trust for granted. However, I do know there are officers who promote climates of implicit bias, "Rank has its privileges," "Do as I say, not as I do," or intimidation, especially when it comes to weight standards, off-duty conduct and behavior, and fidelity. While the military serves as a springboard for equity issues nationally, it certainly has many challenges of its own. The military is pretty private, and most people don't focus on military operations in their daily lives, so a lot of things happen without checks and balances.

What the general public sees are troops fighting and winning our nation's wars. And that's good. Of course, as one might imagine, the fog of war is blinding. But one can easily see—without a magnifying glass, I might add—the inequities in assignments, promotions, command, and flag officer billets for minorities, including Blacks, Asians, Latinos, and women. I've witnessed military officers having their ethnic group changed from Latino to White during promotion board seasons. In my experience, my White colleagues were not concerned with me until I became a threat. As soon as they perceived me being competitive, I was challenged. Most of the military assignments I had were nominative—I had to be nominated and selected. Minority officers didn't receive very many nominative assignments. During my time as a career manager, regarded as a "plum" or "blue-dot" assignment at Human Resources Command (HRC), I oversaw the career development and assignments of thousands of officers, most of whom were White and all of whom were subordinate to me. They circumvented the system often when they didn't like the assignment I selected for them. Officers above me often interfered in the process and made special provisions for those same "golden-boy" officers, usurping my authority and attempting to diminish my credibility at every turn.

Another brazen experience was during my assignment as commandant of the Pacific Command Special Troops Headquarters in Hawaii, with duty throughout the Asia-Pacific region, including Thailand and The Philippines. Prior to my reign, senior officers and NCOs were accustomed to participating in conduct unbecoming of an officer during deployments, like infidelity, misuse of government resources, and often showed blatant disregard for good order and discipline; they were involved in all sorts of unscrupulous engagements. When I refused to accept any of their behavior and conduct, I encountered unbelievable challenges, to include a near physical altercation with a senior officer. I threatened to call the commanding general, who was known for his "no-nonsense" style, to regain command and control. I obviously refused to participate in any such shenanigans, and as a result, I was labeled as arrogant, not a "team-player," and was told, "You're not one of us!" They

were right, I was an officer of character and conviction, I was not "one of them" and didn't want to be! This list of dark experiences goes on and on. Sometimes, it was best to let sleeping dogs lie; I needed no extra attention. I was usually the only Black officer around, and often in positions of notoriety and faced with the prevailing question, "How did you get here? How did you get this assignment? You must know the right people." In their minds, it couldn't have anything to do with me being competent and a "top-performer" who demonstrated unlimited potential for increased responsibilities.

I enjoyed several high-profile assignments. Of particular note are the following: Aide-de-camp, Career Manager, Army's HRC, battery command, joint staff fellow in the pentagon, U.S. Senate Congressional Liaison, speechwriter, and commandant. Though each of these assignments were met with their own unique kind of consternation, I was blessed to experience these types of amazing, challenging, and nominative assignments during my time in service. I believed I was an eagle and was determined I would definitely be all I could be!

That empowering attitude bothered folk. I could write well, I was extraordinarily physically fit, I looked great in my uniform, I was competent, I had a good idea about what right looked like, and my leadership style and energy was infectious. My soldiers performed in an exemplary manner, on and off duty, and their families loved me. I emulated what I wanted to see. Soldiers of other officers loved me too, and I loved them. All that, and my superiors *still* found room for unnecessary critique while my peers weren't even close in competition.

During my first assignment as a commissioned officer, a division artillery commander in South Korea told me, in the presence of another more senior Black officer, "I'd rather have a Black officer working for me because they show up hungry and scared. That fear causes them to prepare and consider risks. White officers, on the other hand, show up privileged and entitled." That conversation has stayed with me for decades, and I've seen the premise of his assertion manifested time and time again. Along the way, I noticed White folk do not like being told "no" or being told what they can and can't do; they rebel fiercely when anyone attempts it. We see that behavior in law enforcement activities, public interactions, customer service, healthcare, and education.

I came to understand, when the rule makers aren't winning, they change the rules—often in the middle of the game. Rule makers often believe the policies aren't meant for them; the rules are meant to contain and maintain the animals in the zoo, not the zookeepers. The challenge for Black folk is we often show up to play baseball following basketball

rules. You gotta fake it 'til you make it. Get in the game, play to win based on the rules. Then, when you attain a seat of influence, change the rules to attain a greater degree of fairness and equality. Too many times, I've personally witnessed rules being broken by the powerful, all in the name of "privilege." Serious infractions were adjudicated in their favor. Those same people suggest Black folk are mostly rule breakers, are lawless, amoral, and don't know how to behave—really? Those fuckin' hypocrites live in glass houses and throw rocks, SMDH □□♂□.

The standards were always different—the goal post changed often. In an early morning breakfast meeting for senior executives, a very prominent *Fortune 500* company executive actually espoused, "The rules are not for us, they are for the ninety-nine percent." My jaw dropped. Wow, was I shocked. That was the first time I realized privilege was real! That privilege is no different in the military—White males make flag officer rank with not just one but two or even *three* DUI charges and multiple extramarital affairs. In other sectors, elected people and sitting justices have committed more egregious violations. A White person even became president of the United States after admitting to grabbing women "by the pussy," SMDH □□♂□!

I sought to be a representative in Congress, a servant-leader for a constituency that has been historically disenfranchised and has not had a seat at the table. They have not had open and fair access to opportunity. Every aspect of our daily lives—schools, healthcare, banking, labor, groceries, housing—hinges on "real politics." It takes a politician to declare we are alive, and a politician to declare we are dead. Have your say!

Unfortunately, there are a growing number of Black politicians who have made it their life's work to "assimilate" and "get alone," practicing the behaviors of those who don't believe the rules apply to them and are lining their pockets on the backs of the very marginalized people they are supposed to be advocating and legislating for. During my congressional campaign, I became quite familiar with politicians who had a passive and slave-like mentality. Because I stopped blindly writing checks and confronted disingenuousness, a Maryland state legislator told people, who she didn't know were my supporters, "We don't want his kind in Maryland politics." When I confronted her, she retreated like the frightened, mendacious, and ill-willed politician she was. I reminded her "my kind" was the kind who sacrificed much during my distinguished military career. "My kind" was the kind who raised two amazing daughters. "My kind" was a man who mentored young Black boys and positively impacted their lives. "My kind" was a man who generously contributed to her campaign. "My kind" committed himself to a lifetime of public service! Damned coward—she was a prime example of morass and a cheerleader of exploiting Black folk.

It is because of my lived experiences as a single dad raising two Black daughters, my faith, my trials and tribulations, my willingness to seek mental health treatment, my authentic associations, my service in and out of the Army's uniform as a senior leader in the executive branch, and as a congressional staffer in the legislative branch, that I gained incremental courage.

My life's work has been, and is still, about being in the service to others. Being a mentor and a coach to young Black boys and other boys of color who are hurting is paramount to that service. I'm not sure if we are prepared for the consequences of not meeting their needs. We've seen some snippets of what that looks like. Too many shootings, too much domestic violence, homelessness, drug additions, unemployment, truancy, police brutality, and a disproportionate number of Black people incarcerated (approximately 14 percent of the population, but over 40 percent of the prison population, WTF?!!! *SMDH* □□♂□□). When you make the time to pay attention, it's quite easy to see these communities, where folk have lost hope! When people lose hope and are left to survive by any means necessary, real anarchy becomes inevitable. We've seen it in St. Louis and Los Angeles. We've seen it in Chicago, New York City, and Baltimore. My work now is laser-focused because of what I've been exposed to, and because I have such a strong desire to stand in the gap and be strong for those people who are not strong enough to stand up and speak up for themselves.

I am passionate about serving people and being a leader. I am passionate about being a dad and shaping the minds of two very talented and beautiful daughters. I'm very passionate about pouring into the lives of young Black males who are struggling to survive. I'm very passionate about service and leadership. When I consider that someone taught me how to serve and how to lead, I'm inspired to keep going. I'm standing on the shoulders of ancestors—giants who paid with their lives for me to do what I do. People died hellacious deaths so I could serve and wear a uniform. People died painful deaths so I could get an education and gain knowledge in American schools. People died painful deaths so I could work as an executive in the executive branch and as a staffer in the legislative branch. People even died so I could be a dad and so I could write a book. I'm talking about my ancestors. They were Black men and women who endured atrocities, tragedies, and a genocide equal to or greater than what the Jewish, Japanese, and European people endured combined—I shall never forget! There are few people on Earth who have endured more than the trials and tribulations of Black folk—very few!

I am motivated to be courageous—to stand boldly even if it means I pay with my life. I can't get tired, because had our ancestors gotten tired, buses would still be segregated today. We still wouldn't be able to drink out of the same water fountains as Caucasians. We still wouldn't be able to live in the communities we choose in America. If my ancestors had gotten tired, I wouldn't have been able to serve in the military. What motivates me most are my ancestors and their sacrifices, their strength, courage, and fortitude. I can't get tired because they didn't get tired, and they are depending on me to help carry their legacy. I can't let their works be in vain.

I am still on my journey, and I still haven't gotten it right every time. If I could change a few things, I would. I would make much better choices about the people I invited into my life—I would choose friends much more carefully, remembering the words of my Madea when she said, "You think all these people are your friends. When the dust settles, you'll be able to count your true friends on one hand." I would pay closer attention to people showing me who they are and trust my instincts and gift of discernment. I wouldn't put much stock in what people say—I'd pay vigorous attention to what they do! I would do things differently in my marriage. I would work to be more vulnerable and a stronger communicator and confront my issues and challenges head-on. I would fight harder to maintain my family unit. I would love without boundaries, I'd dance like nobody was watching, and I would laugh too much, LOL □.

Life isn't like a box of chocolates; you *do* know what you're gonna get. You know by the seeds you plant and the type of energy you deliver. You know by the words you speak and the deeds you do. These ideals lead me to the deep appreciation I have for the scripture, "that you may be children of your Father in heaven. He causes his sun to rise on the evil and the good and sends rain on the righteous and the unrighteous" (Matthew 5:45 [NIV]).

To my mind's eye, the key is to continue moving forward; allow God to order your steps and guide your spirit in His ordained purpose for your life.

I live by the mantra, "Each one, reach one, teach one." My life is not my own. God has ordained my life for a purpose. I must continue to walk in my God-given purpose and make sure I share what God has blessed me with. God didn't bless me to hoard the blessing; He blessed me to share. If being courageous was easy, everybody would exercise courage.

It is not in comfort we grow. It is through challenging our brains and our spiritual muscles that we gain strength. My assertions, suggestions, and my experiences will hopefully help people to reflect and consider another perspective. If you are offended, great. Now, ask yourself why you are offended. Challenge what you think you know. Challenge yourself to unlearn a few things; learning is a lifelong process.

I've shared my experiences. They are unembellished, and I consciously made no attempt to hide the truth. When folk become defensive about an issue, please pay attention. When facts are highlighted, they speak for themselves. There are no alternatives.

We are indeed entitled to our own set of opinions, but not our own set of facts. It took a lot of courage for me to share many aspects of my personal journey. For a long time, I was too ashamed, too afraid, and too deceitful to share. Though I was abandoned at birth, made to repeat 5th grade, experienced trauma associated with being in the Pentagon on 911, divorced, struggled with my sexuality, discriminated against in the military, counted out, marginalized, diagnosed with afflictions associated with my military service, lost two elections, embarrassed, talked about, had people to walk out of my life [thank you, lawdy!]—they tried to bury me, but they didn't know I am the seed! I am *enough*! I would rather be running, but even if I have to jump or crawl, I'm moving forward. I leap from the shoulders of giants who came before me, and I shall not let their works be in vain. Every good thing God says I am, I am! I speak creation because I have become courageous incrementally.

I've taken back my power, I've revealed my shame, and I'm being the eagle God created me to be. That was a process—I was on the potter's wheel for a long time, and I'm bound to be again as I keep on moving on. I was the clay: wet, kneaded, pulled, stretched, shaped, and placed in the fire, adorned with a finishing polish, and fired some more. Weeping may endure for a night, but oh, in the morning, joy cometh. For the first time in my life, I have peace that surpasses all understanding; I shall not be moved!

Maybe you're not Black. Maybe you have controversial ideas. Maybe you're a woman, autistic, not privileged, Muslim, Mexican, or LGBTQ+. Whoever you are, seek the courage to be bold, to be *you*, and be unapologetic about it! I'm reminded of advice from my Madea: "Whatever you do, do your very best, and be the best while you're doing it!"

Chapter Summary

❖ Choose to grow—challenge yourself. Struggle is real; validate it, then move on.

❖ Each one, reach one, teach one.

❖ Demand a seat at the table. Power relinquishes nothing without demand.

❖ Be wise, choose your battles, and speak your

truth.

❖ I prayed, I believed, I received—in time. I believed God would take me far, far away—and he did.

❖ I did my work; tough work to reset my mindset.

❖ When the rules change unexpectedly, adjust and continue moving forward.

❖ Being tired is not an option. "Laziness is nothing more than the habit of resting before you get tired" (Jules Renard).

❖ People say a lot—pay attention to what they *do*!

❖ Rain falls on the just and unjust.

❖ You matter and you are important. There will never be another you.

www.ingramcontent.com/pod-product-compliance
Lightning Source LLC
LaVergne TN
LVHW051051080426
835508LV00019B/1825